W9-BZX-982

"A must read for all funders. The authors have rightfully challenged us to develop the capacity of our own organizations at the same time we should be supporting nonprofits in their efforts to have higher performing operations and a greater social impact on their communities."

Patty Burness, Executive Director
Gib Myers, Chairman
Entrepreneurs' Foundation, Menlo Park, CA

"This book is at the top of my reading wish list for nonprofit trustees and managers. Letts, Ryan, and Grossman have written the most important book yet on creating a culture of performance."

William M. Dietel, Chairman
National Center for Nonprofit Boards

"*High Performance Nonprofit Organizations* is required reading for social sector leaders and students of comparative management. This well-written volume presents a rigorous summary of critical management practices, illuminated by action-oriented insights from leading businesses and nonprofits—all aimed at achieving uncommon performance."

Richard E. Cavanaugh
President and Chief Executive Officer
The Conference Board

"If high burn-out in the nonprofit world has been the problem, then *High Performance Nonprofit Organizations* is the answer. This book provides marvelous insight into the underlying reasons of why nonprofit managers continually end up in a situation of trying to do too much with too few resources. It gives well-grounded solutions for avoiding this trap, based on examples from the for-profit sector, and demonstrates how nonprofit organizations can develop a solid, yet dynamic infrastructure from which to deliver their mission. If more funders, executive directors, and board members embraced the tenets of this book then we just might encounter a revolution among nonprofit organizations and the millions of institutions and individuals they affect."

Carolyn Bess, Executive Director
Outdoor Explorations, Inc.

NONPROFIT LAW, FINANCE, AND MANAGEMENT SERIES

High Performance Nonprofit Organizations

Managing Upstream for Greater Impact

Christine W. Letts
William P. Ryan
Allen Grossman

John Wiley & Sons, Inc.

New York • Chichester • Weinheim • Brisbane • Singapore • Toronto

Copyright© 1999 by John Wiley & Sons, Inc. All rights reserved.

Published simultaneously in Canada.

Library of Congress Cataloging-in-Publication Data

Letts, Christine.
   High performance nonprofit organizations: managing upstream for greater impact / Christine Letts, William Ryan, Allen Grossman.
     p.   cm.
   Includes bibliographical references and index.
   ISBN 0-471-17457-2 (cloth : alk. paper)
    1. Nonprofit organizations—Management   I. Ryan, William P.
II. Grossman, Allen.   III. Title.
HD62.6.L47   1998
658'.048—dc21   98-24240

Printed in the United States of America.

10 9 8 7 6 5 4

About the Authors

Christine W. Letts is a lecturer in public policy and executive director of the Hauser Center for Nonprofit Organizations at Harvard. She has extensive experience in private and public management. At the Kennedy School of Government, Letts teaches courses and executive education in nonprofit management, general public management, and organizational change. As the executive director of the Hauser Center, she is responsible for coordinating activities related to building nonprofit curriculum, research, and executive education for nonprofit leaders. Research interests include organizational performance in nonprofit organizations and the impact of funding practices on nonprofit capacity. Before joining the Kennedy School, she served in the cabinet of Governor Evan Bayh of Indiana. Prior to that she was a vice president in manufacturing for Cummins Engine Co. Letts holds an MBA from Harvard Business School.

William P. Ryan is a Cambridge-based consultant specializing in strategies to strengthen the performance of nonprofit organizations. His research, analysis, and program development help both nonprofits and foundations develop capacity-building strategies that respond to organizational and sector-wide challenges. He is currently investigating the growth of for-profit social service providers, the emergence of alternative nonprofit governance strategies, and the prospects for value-added grantmaking. His current clients and project partners include the Rockefeller Foundation, Pew Charitable Trusts, Hauser Center for Nonprofit Organizations at Harvard, and Family Service America. He received a B.A. in religion from

Columbia University and a M.P.A. from the Kennedy School of Government, Harvard University.

Allen Grossman is a senior lecturer of business administration at the Harvard Business School and a visiting scholar at the Harvard Graduate School of Education. He served as president and chief executive officer of Outward Bound USA for 6 years before stepping down in 1997 to work exclusively on the challenges of creating high-performing nonprofit organizations and the relationship between a nonprofit's management and its social impact. Before joining the nonprofit sector, he served as a regional chief executive of Albert Fisher PLC and chairman of the board of Grossman Paper Company, a national distributor of packaging products. During this period, Mr. Grossman served on and chaired a number of nonprofit boards. He received a B.S. in corporate finance from the University of Pennsylvania's Wharton School.

Acknowledgments

We are grateful to the advisory group that helped organize and launch the Going to Scale Project, which has culminated in this book: Thomas E. Backer, Human Interaction Research Institute: Joel L. Fleishman, Sanford Institute of Public Policy, Duke University; Peter Goldmark, formerly of the Rockefeller Foundation; Michael Rubinger, formerly of the Pew Charitable Trusts; Terry Saario, formerly of Northwest Area Foundation; Dorothy Stoneman, Youth-Build USA; and Mitchell Sviridoff.

We are most grateful to the many people who participated in our roundtables and other discussion groups: John Anderson, New American Schools; P. Jefferson Armistead, Local Initiatives Support Corporation; William A. Baker, The Village for Families and Children; Jeffrey Bradach, Graduate School of Business, Harvard University; Gail Breslow, The Computer Clubhouse; David Brown, Boston Ballet; Nordhal Brue, Bruegger's Bagels; Thomas Bushman, Executive Service Corps; William D. Bygrave, Center for Entrepreneurial Studies, Babson College: Michael Caslin III, National Foundation for Teaching Entrepreneurship; Walter Channing, CW Group; Lisa G. Chapnick, consultant; J. Gregory Dees, Stanford University; Alison Friedman, Au Bon Pain; Marion Fremont-Smith, Choate, Hall & Stewart; Reed Henderson, Family Service America; Robert F. Higgins, Highland Capital Fund; James R. Hines, Jr., University of Michigan; Alice Howard, Vista Consulting; Ruth Irving-Parham, YWCA of Boston; Jan Jaffe, Ford Foundation; Warren Jeffries, Xerox Corporation; T. Meriwether Jones, Aspen Institute; Roger King, consultant; Vanessa Kirsch, Public Allies; and Daniel Levinthal, Wharton School, University of Pennsylvania.

Thanks also to Marc Lindenberg, CARE; Lois Loofbourrow, Summerbridge National; Terry Ann Lunt, International Health Specialists, Inc.; Pamela Lynam, MD, AVSC International; Brooke Mahoney, Volunteer Consulting Group; Bruce Marks, Boston Ballet; John Marks, Search for Common Ground; Ruth McCambridge, Management Consulting Services; Kristen McCormack, former CEO, United Neighborhood Houses; Nesly Metayer, Common Ground Project; Francis K. Moseley, Boys & Girls Clubs of Boston; J. Louis Newell, The Boston Company; P. Ranganath Nayak, The Boston Consulting Group; Thomas L.P. O'Donnell, Ropes & Gray; Gregg Petersmeyer, Indiana University Center on Philanthropy; Robin Purcell, Hewlett-Packard Company; Melinda Rabb, Professor, Brown University, Philanthropist; David Racine, Replication and Program Strategies, Inc.; Darrell Ross, Ritz-Carlton Hotel Company, Inc.; Eric Schwarz, Citizens Schools, Inc.; Nancy Schwoyer, Wellspring House, Inc.; James E. Shipp, Cummins Metropower, Inc.; Edward Skloot, Surdna Foundation; Lisa Smith, Robin Hood Foundation; Jeffrey A. Snider, Paula Financial; Helen Spaulding, Trustee/Philanthropist; Cynthia Steele, AVSC International; Christopher Stone, Vera Institute of Justice, Inc.; Jae-Ho Synn, MacTemps, Inc.; F. Morgan Taylor III, Philanthropist; E.B. Wilson, Executive Service Corps of New England; and Dennis Yao, Wharton School, University of Pennsylvania.

As background for the inquiry, we had the benefit of four going-to-scale case studies, prepared by Michael Bailin, now of the Edna McConnell Clark Foundation; William Grinker; Elizabeth Reisner, Policy Studies Associates, Inc.; and Lou Winnick, Fund for the City of New York.

We appreciate the funding of the Rockefeller Foundation and Pew Charitable Trusts in support of this project. Jane Leu and Mary Nell Wegner provided critical research and organizational support. Jane Grossman was a diligent reviewer of countless drafts. Ken White brought a sharp editorial eye and excellent research skills to the preparation of the final manuscript. Mark Moore, Kennedy School of Government, Harvard University, provided important criticism and feedback. At The Philanthropic Initiative, Catherine Corinha provided outstanding project administration support and Peter Karoff provided valuable counsel and encouragement.

Contents

Contents

Introduction

The nonprofit sector is filled with great ideas and thoughtful, caring people. In many ways, it represents our collective best inclinations: generosity, inclusivity, and determined optimism. The nonprofit sector attempts to bridge the many gaps in our society by bringing people together, proposing alternatives, advocating for change, and implementing remedies. In the course of providing extensive benefits to a diverse range of people and communities, it produces remarkably innovative programs. As one of the underpinnings of American society, the nonprofit sector has built an enduring legacy of community and service.

The nonprofit world thrives on impossible challenges. Achieving every goal articulated in the sector would mean the perfection of the human condition (or a hopeless tangle of competing visions!). So it's not surprising that nonprofit organizations, and the sector as a whole, continually fall short of lofty expectations. But as the nonprofit sector increases in both size and importance, so does the task of addressing those many challenges more effectively.

The nonprofit sector encompasses a vast range of organizations, from health-care giants and universities, to nationwide member-serving groups like the Girl Scouts, to advocacy groups like Common Cause and National Right to Life, to religious orders, to an array of locally based associations of every description. A rich variety of organizational structures and practices have developed under the nonprofit umbrella, and government, foundations, members, and individual donors in every conceivable combination fund the sector's activities. The nonprofit sector now accounts for about 8 percent of the gross domestic product and 7 percent of total employment, with an annual payroll of $480 billion.[1] In addition to the 9.6 million people employed by the sector, millions of volunteers work billions of hours annually in virtually every part of the sector.[2]

The nonprofit sector faces an increasingly complex set of pressures. Perhaps in response to its growing visibility, some critics are challenging the value that nonprofits generate in return for their tax-advantaged status, and ever-present questions about results have a new gravity. As economist Lester Salamon puts it, the sector faces a "crisis of effectiveness."[3] At the same time, the boundaries between sectors have become more permeable as nonprofits refine their fee-for-service structures and create for-profit spinoffs, and the for-profit sector finds potential payoffs in the nonprofit domain. For example, for-profit organizations have moved aggressively into government-funded social services (such as education, child care, health care, elder services, programs for at-risk youth, and employment training and placement), where nonprofits generate a significant share of their revenues from government contracts. In their hearts, funders and governments may honor traditional nonprofit values of service and compassion, but in their contracts they are demanding efficient, cost-effective services of consistent quality.[4]

Nonprofits that lack the capacity to adapt will suffer in this changing environment. As the sector matures and the environment around it changes, nonprofit leaders—whether CEOs, boards, managers, staff, volunteers, entrepreneurs, or researchers—must seek out new ways to increase the effectiveness of their programs, organizations, and missions.

FULFILLING THE PROMISE OF THE NONPROFIT SECTOR

This book grows out of an inquiry into the prospects for expanding successful programs so they can create large-scale social impact. It originated as informal conversation among nonprofit and foundation leaders who were all struggling with the challenges of going to scale. The group included Peter Goldmark, formerly of the Rockefeller Foundation; Michael Rubinger, formerly of the Pew Charitable Trusts; and Mitchell Sviridoff, formerly of the Ford Foundation; Dorothy Stoneman, the founder of the fast-growing YouthBuild

USA; and Allen Grossman, who instigated the conversation to help him manage the expansion of Outward Bound USA's successful education-reform initiative (and went on to preside over this two-year inquiry). Allen was joined in managing the project by Bill Ryan, a consultant to nonprofits and foundations, and Christine Letts, lecturer in public management and executive director of the Hauser Center for Nonprofit Organizations at Harvard University. This group expanded its conversations into a series of seminars that engaged additional nonprofit leaders, business managers from the private sector, and specialists in a number of disciplines.

The inquiry concludes not with a silver-bullet solution, but with a fundamental redefinition of the challenge—from the most prevalent conception of the challenge, as one of expanding effective *programs*, to a new formulation of the challenge, as one of building effective *organizations* that can sustain and improve those programs. Traditionally, nonprofits have relied on programs to create impact, and on expanding those programs to increase the reach of organizations and missions. Both funders and nonprofits are increasingly recognizing that sometimes even the best programs do not survive, much less grow, a phenomenon recently explored by Lisbeth B. Schorr. She revisited, after several years, the successful youth programs originally profiled in her 1989 book *Within Our Reach*, only to discover that a number of them had ceased operating or appeared less effective.[5] Although a variety of forces threaten success in the nonprofit world, one fact is clear: Programs cannot stand alone. Even innovative programs alone are a weak foundation for large-scale social impact.

The capacity for strong performance in organizations *provides the foundation for lasting social benefits.*

The missing ingredient in the prevalent, program-centered conception of social impact is organizational capacity. Programs need solid organizations behind them—organizations focused on fulfilling a mission in a changing environment. Organizations not only develop programs, but also operate, sustain, improve, and grow them—eventually replacing them with new approaches. It is the capacity for strong performance in organizations—the ability to develop, sustain, and improve the delivery of a mission—that provides the foundation for lasting social benefits.

As banal as this principle may seem, the nonprofit sector appears highly ambivalent about strengthening its organizations. On the one hand, everyone can agree that we need to take care of the organizations that are tackling difficult problems. On the other hand, deeply ingrained behaviors, public policy, funding systems, and the culture of nonprofit service itself have all led the sector to rely on virtually anything *but* organizational capacity as a foundation for lasting effectiveness.

Perhaps there are good reasons why nonprofit leaders have tended to shy away from building organizational capacity. After all, the nonprofit sector has always prided itself on meeting "dual bottom lines": financial accountability (narrowly defined as meeting budgets and spending responsibly) and social gains (broadly defined as advancing a given mission). In addition to delivering services, nonprofits create more general benefits, by bringing concerned people together in pursuit of a larger good. These multiple agendas may have pushed organizational performance into the background. With this book we hope to move it toward center stage.

A CROSS-SECTOR LOOK AT PERFORMANCE

To gain perspective on the issue of nonprofit effectiveness, we began studying for-profit and nonprofit practices side by side. This cross-sector approach looked promising for two reasons. First, examining nonprofit issues in relief against another sector helps identify how the nonprofit environment influences the decisions and behaviors of managers and practitioners. It can produce what has been called "bisociation"—wherein compelling new insights emerge when dissimilar things are compared. In studying a number of exciting cases, we believe the inquiry has generated new angles on pressing problems. Second, businesses are generally dedicated to growth, which was how we initially conceived of the challenge of increasing social impact. From this angle it seemed that a cross-sector inquiry could uncover techniques, methods, or perspectives that might be useful to nonprofits that wanted to expand their programs or organizations.

Despite these promising possibilities, a cross-sector approach carries negative connotations for many in the nonprofit sector. Too often, comparisons to businesses are used as a weapon to indict nonprofits for incompetence, instead of as a tool for promoting learning and change. The crudest of these comparisons comes in the form of a conversation-stopping lecture that begins: *"If this place were run like a business. . ."* Some nonprofit leaders resist a cross-sector approach because they are dedicated to solving problems they believe are *caused* by corporate practices or market failures. Why model a nonprofit after socially destructive enterprises? Still others are offended by the creeping commercialism that has made advertising ubiquitous and materialism the highest value. Finally, some dismiss business methods because "business performance" as a generic proposition is a myth; they point to incompetence and corruption all around, from defense contractors to the savings and loans debacle.

> *The crudest of these comparisons comes in the form of a conversation-stopping lecture that begins:* "If this place were run like a business. . . ."

Our interest—far from creating invidious comparisons—is to see whether and how business methods could be adapted, or already have been adapted, to support nonprofit goals. The potential of this approach, notes Melinda Rabb, a nonprofit board member, is to "adapt *their* best practices to make *our* product—our organizations and our community—as compelling to as many people as possible." For those who live and breathe nonprofit work, the chance to see our sector from a more distant vantage point offers new clarity on the challenges facing the sector.

FINDING THE RIGHT QUESTIONS

As our inquiry unfolded, we began looking at the challenge of social impact very differently. We eventually arrived at two questions that focus on organizational performance as a critical and overlooked dimension of social impact.

1. *Reframing the question from "How do programs expand?" to "How do organizations perform?"*

Having started out equating "greater social impact" with "expanding programs," we wanted to explore the growth and expansion practices of businesses to see if they could be adapted for use by nonprofits. But very early on in discussions about growth strategies, more fundamental aspects of performance ended up dominating the conversation. The capacity for growth, we heard, is not discrete, and is more likely embedded in other organizational capacities. Organizations that grow and sustain themselves successfully make a series of choices before, during, and after their expansion. Growth, it seems, takes much more than a growth strategy.

Instead of focusing on program growth and replication, we began pursuing broader questions about the issues that influence success and sustainability at any scale: How do successful organizations learn? How do they measure and improve their performance? How do they innovate and then adapt to remain relevant to changing markets? So we revised the question "How do programs expand?" to "How do organizations perform?" In the process, we reshaped our inquiry into one about organizational capacity. Specifically, we decided to examine a series of management practices and organizational processes that can help nonprofits better serve their missions.

2. *The critical follow-up question: "What enables organizations to perform well?"*

Our discussions with practitioners from the nonprofit and for-profit sectors focused first on the question of whether a given organizational process was relevant to nonprofits. We found that

managers in both sectors used similar processes for the same reasons. For example, we heard the manager of a multinational electronics company and the executive of a small social-service agency
discuss their use of very similar human resource strategies for
improving performance, and managers from a luxury hotel-chain
and a homeless shelter compare their methods for assessing and
improving the quality of their services. We believe their methods
and choices hold important lessons for other nonprofit managers
and boards trying to expand the capacity of their organizations.
This book, in part, is a catalog of best practices that nonprofit managers can use to improve the performance of their organizations.

In addition to the question of how relevant these practices are,
the cross-sector stories raised questions about how accessible they
are to managers in each sector: What environmental factors enable
organizations to perform well? What are the external factors—the
market forces (or their equivalents), funding systems and public
policies—that encourage performance? What are the internal characteristics—the resources, talents, systems, and processes of the
organization and its staff—that support strong performance? The
differences that emerged in exploring these questions begin to illuminate why the nonprofit sector has a relatively shallow capacity
for building the good organizations needed to develop and sustain
good programs. We also began to see the outlines of an agenda for
developing organizational capacity in the nonprofit sector, and supporting strong performance as the foundation for lasting social benefits.

3. *Developing an organizational approach to performance*

These questions—"How do organizations perform?" and "What
enables them to perform?"—then formed the core of our approach.
To answer them, we convened a series of roundtable discussions
with managers from both sectors (including many who worked in
both businesses and nonprofits, as well as in government) for discussions at the Kennedy School of Government at Harvard University. In each session we focused on a single process that could help
improve organizational performance. Managers from both sectors
presented cases outlining how they managed a given process, and

the discussion then focused on what internal and external practices influenced their performance. The processes we explored related to some of the most fundamental organizational goals of learning, measuring and improving performance, and motivating people. We looked at generic processes to advance these important functions. Nothing in this book is based on trade-marked, off-the-shelf consulting products.

Although we offer a number of cases and examples to explore how organizational capacity can help advance the mission of an organization, we do not present any of these organizations as all-around exemplars of high performance. They may excel in one area and lag in others. Instead of advancing model organizations, we want to disaggregate the processes that drive good performance and consider how relevant and accessible they are for nonprofits.

THE CHALLENGE FOR NONPROFIT LEADERS, BOARDS, AND FUNDERS

Unfortunately, as we will argue, building organizational capacity in the nonprofit sector is not rewarded or encouraged by a marketplace as it is in the for-profit sector. It will therefore require the willful effort of nonprofit managers, board members, and funders to increase expectations for and investment in organizational performance. Difficult? Yes. Unrealistic? No more than accomplishing any of the difficult items on the nonprofit sector's social agenda: reducing poverty, improving health, enriching arts and culture, or protecting the environment. What seems unrealistic is attempting to accomplish these goals without a clear and profound commitment to strengthening nonprofit organizations.

USING THIS BOOK

The book is organized in three parts. In Part I, the role of organizational performance in the nonprofit sector is discussed. In Chapter 1, we discuss in more depth why organizational capacity—especially the learning, innovating, and improvement functions that comprise what we call *adaptive capacity*—is an essential, but overlooked resource for achieving social impact in the nonprofit sector. In Chapter 2, the findings of our cross-sector survey of organizational processes are summarized—revealing that even when nonprofit managers try to use organizational processes to improve performance they face a number of special obstacles.

In Part II, we explore chapter-by-chapter, four organizational processes that nonprofit organizations can and sometimes do use to improve their performance:

- *Quality processes*—to continuously review the quality of services and to generate improvements that will benefit clients.

- *Product development*—to maximize the chances for creating effective program ideas by tapping the talents of employees throughout the organization, supporting the passion and creativity of staff, and studying the needs of clients intensively.

- *Benchmarking*—to identify and implement the best practices that respond to an organization's particular learning and improvement needs.

- *Human resources management*—to attract, motivate, and develop employees to advance the organization's goals and mission.

These chapters include brief case studies from our roundtable series showing how both nonprofit and for-profit managers use each process. The cases are presented not so much as how-to guides, but as illustrations of the special challenges of building organizational capacity in the nonprofit sector.

In Part III, we explore how other nonprofit stakeholders, not just managers, create an environment that raises both support for and expectations about organizational performance. Again using the cross-sector roundtables as the starting point, we consider the role of three important stakeholders:

- *Boards.* As board members with experience in both sectors suggest, the nonprofit board can lead the way in creating support for developing organizational performance—but must first shift its thinking about performance.

9

- *The National Office.* The national office of multi-site operations in both sectors is heavily involved in growing programs, but may find the challenge of expanding to new sites relatively easy compared to the challenge of sustaining performance and impact among front-line operators.
- *Funders.* As a comparison of venture-capital investment and foundation grantmaking practices shows, funders can combine their investments with organization-building assistance to ensure the success of those they support.

In the conclusion, we propose the development of a new nonprofit agenda to advance organizational performance.

Ultimately, we aim to provoke more discussion, more research, and more action on the challenges of building organizational capacity. This book is by no means an attempt to have the definitive last word on these challenges. To the contrary, we hope to use this practitioner-based research and analysis to open a wider, deeper discussion about performance for the social good.

ADDITIONAL READING

Drucker, Peter F. *Managing the Nonprofit Organization: Practices and Principles.* New York: HarperCollins, 1990.

Heifetz, Ronald A. *Leadership Without Easy Answers.* Cambridge, MA: Harvard University Press, 1994.

Lipsky, Michael and Steven Smith. *Nonprofits for Hire: The Welfare State in the Age of Contracting.* Cambridge, MA: Harvard University Press, 1993.

Martin, Lawrence L. and Peter M. Kettner. *Measuring the Performance of Human Service Programs.* Thousand Oaks, CA: Sage Publications, 1996.

Moore, Mark. *Creating Public Value.* Cambridge, MA: Harvard University Press, 1995.

Oster, Sharon. *Strategic Management for Nonprofit Organizations: Theory and Cases.* New York: Oxford University Press, 1995.

Schorr, Lisbeth B. *Common Purpose*. New York: Anchor Books/Doubleday, 1997.

Wolf, Tom. *Managing a Nonprofit Organization*. New York: Simon & Schuster, 1990.

ENDNOTES

[1]Independent Sector, *The Nonprofit Almanac* (San Francisco: Jossey-Bass, 1996).

[2]Virginia Ann Hodgkinson and Murray S. Weitzman, *Giving and Volunteering in the United States 1996 Edition* (Washington, DC: Independent Sector, 1996).

[3]Lester M. Salamon, *Holding the Center: America's Nonprofit Sector at the Crossroads* (New York: Nathan Cummings Foundation, 1997).

[4]Peter M. Kettner and Lawrence L. Martin, "Performance Management: The New Accountability," *Administration in Social Work*, Vol. 21 (1), 1997.

[5]She also discovered programs that were thriving, and describes in *Common Purpose* some of the characteristics of successful programs. Lisbeth B. Schorr, *Common Purpose* (New York: Anchor Books/Doubleday, 1997).

PART I

Connecting Organizational Capacity, Performance, and Social Impact

CHAPTER ONE

Organizational Performance: The Hidden Engine of Social Impact

FRAMING QUESTIONS

▶ How does organizational capacity support performance?

▶ How are program impact and organizational capacity linked?

▶ Does organizational capacity improve the performance of small nonprofits?

The biggest challenge many in the nonprofit sector face is sustaining or expanding successful programs. They have designed, piloted, and evaluated a number of effective programs, and want to move them to large-scale implementation. This challenge has stirred intense interest in replication and expansion strategies, and a fair amount of frustration, as people discover how difficult it is to sustain and expand the success of promising programs. There is another way to look at sustained, large-scale impact—not as a function of program design alone, but of program design and organizational performance together. Behind every effective program, and especially every *sustained* effective program, is an organization that

15

performs well. The challenge of large-scale impact, then, can be re-formulated as the challenge of helping more nonprofits perform better.

To understand how organizational performance can drive program outcomes, and how the nonprofit sector can support better performance, means looking anew at the issue of organizational capacity. For nonprofits, organizational capacity has been so narrowly interpreted that it appeals only to management enthusiasts and technical specialists. But beyond the essential basics of financial control and project management—where nonprofits tend to draw the boundary of organizational capacity—are a set of broader, deeper, more vital organizational capacities that drive performance. Understanding these capacities can fundamentally reshape how individual nonprofits succeed in delivering on their missions and how the sector approaches the challenge of supporting large-scale social impact.

CURRENT STRATEGIES FOR SOCIAL IMPACT: PROGRAM, PROGRAM, PROGRAM

In the most prevalent strategies for sustaining large-scale impact (also known in short-hand as "going-to-scale"), programs are the center of the universe. They are considered the real generators of value—the things that work—and the starting point for all strategies to improve effectiveness. One useful analysis of these strategies comes from international development, where practitioners and academics have generated a small but illuminating literature on the issue. Michael Edwards and David Hulme have identified three types of scaling-up strategies, which describe fairly well the thinking and strategies of U.S. nonprofit stakeholders as well:[1]

1. *Expansion* strategies seek to create *more programs* or *bigger organizations*, and take scale literally as a matter of size. Program replication is the premier expansion strategy in the United States. It holds the promise of many different organizations implementing an effective program in a consistent manner.

An alternative expansion strategy would be to expand an organization itself so it can deliver a program in new sites.

2. *Diffusion* strategies rely on the *formal or spontaneous spread* of a program or idea. Efforts to disseminate lessons from the work of nonprofits and funders have garnered increasing attention in recent years. Most of these efforts promote best practices, share lessons learned, or publicize innovations—particularly through awards programs, conferences, and publications. A few nonprofits and foundations have encouraged the closer study of the dynamics of dissemination as part of their efforts to scale-up successful programs.[2]

3. *Policy reform* strategies do not focus directly on growth, but achieve impact through *deliberate influence, networking, policy, and legal reform.* By changing the rules of the game, policy reform strategies may even obviate the need for a program that addresses a specific problem by getting at root causes. For example, after first offering a teen parenting course, a nonprofit might switch its attention to preventing teen pregnancy: influencing how reproductive health is taught in schools, or the availability of constructive activities for youth.

In various combinations, these strategies can significantly enhance the prospects for large-scale social impact. Yet the search for scale is still on: These strategies have not yielded as much impact as program proponents have hoped. (See Exhibit 1-1.)

Existing			*Needed*
Expansion	*Diffusion*	*Policy Reform*	*Organizational Capacity*
Create more programs/enlarge organization	Spread ideas informally/ share best practices	Change the rules/address underlying issues	Rethink practices/ change the environment

Exhibit 1–1   Strategies for increasing impact.

AN OVERLOOKED STRATEGY FOR SOCIAL IMPACT: HIGH-PERFORMING ORGANIZATIONS

In large part, the problem with these program-centered strategies is that they limit discourse and problem-solving to one dimension— program design and expansion. They undervalue the vital role that organizational performance plays in creating social impact. At some level, every practitioner knows there is more to effective outcomes than a program design, and what we praise as "innovative programs" are often just "well-implemented" programs. For example, how many youth development programs that rely on empowerment or building self-esteem actually differ from each other in design? How many education reform strategies actually depart significantly from the principles established by Dewey at the turn of the century? The programs that stand out as remarkable are often the ones that are remarkably well implemented. It is performance, not program design alone, that makes the difference. But lacking the interest in or vocabulary to describe organizational performance, much of the nonprofit sector continues to look to programs as the key determinant of good outcomes.

> *"Innovative" often means little more than "well implemented."*

In a study of innovation in the public and nonprofit sectors, Paul Light illuminates another aspect of this dynamic. The social sector, he argues, focuses too much on *innovation* and not enough on *innovativeness*—the capacity to innovate repeatedly.[3] For example, he observes that the Ford Foundation–Kennedy School Innovations Award program focuses on innovative programs—their design and technology. Publicizing the winning innovations may lead to replication in other places, and may encourage other organizations to risk innovation. However, it provides less insight into the *process* by which the organization created its program, how it could be sustained, and how future innovations will be nurtured. In contrast, the private-sector Malcolm Baldridge Quality Award focuses not only on a quality product, but also on the *capacity of the organization* to create and sustain quality in all its work.

> *The social sector focuses too much on* innovation *and not enough on* innovativeness—*the capacity to innovate repeatedly.*

It's not only the nonprofit sector that faces the challenge of linking organizational performance and program design. Says New York City schools chancellor Rudy Crew, on efforts to reform the city's school system:

Creating one or even a dozen good schools has never been difficult. . . . The challenge for urban educators isn't building more pilot programs, but finding a way to replicate—or in education parlance, to "scale up"—select reforms to create an entire system that works. . . . The real question for urban America is, 'Can you replicate it, can you do it in a cost-effective way and can you create the organizational culture that gives rise to it on a scale that impacts the lives of every child in the system?'[4]

Crew's approach and the Baldridge award criteria both underscore the fact that focusing on program design and expansion alone (or on policy reform to support better, bigger programs) will not create widespread social impact. Social impact rests just as critically on the even more difficult processes of *creating and sustaining high performance in the organizations* that implement the programs. Whether originating a new program, replicating someone else's innovative program, or attempting to influence policy to preclude the need for a program, the organization's ability to perform well is decisive. Ultimately, large-scale impact requires large-scale performance.

ORGANIZATIONAL CAPACITY: THE MEANS FOR HIGH PERFORMANCE

This performance-centered conception of impact leads in turn to the question of organizational capacity. Specifically, how do nonprofits build their capacity for performance? Depending on their goals and sophistication, effective nonprofit organizations rely on three types of organizational capacity (see Exhibit 1-2). The first two—the capacities for program delivery and program expansion—are already familiar to nonprofits and their funders. But it is the third type, what we call adaptive capacity, that makes an organization not only efficient but also effective. The capacities function in distinct ways:[5]

Program Delivery Capacity

This is the starting point in any nonprofit's effort to create impact, where knowledge of a given field and analysis of a given problem or social challenge lead to a program. Program delivery capacity therefore often grows directly out of a specialized field of practice or a profession (e.g., public health, education, environmental science, or sociology). Here, performance is a matter of program efficacy: The program can be studied to determine whether it produces the intended outcomes (e.g., in fewer teen pregnancies, safer neighborhoods, or improved student test scores). For advocacy organizations, "program" usually takes the form of research, analysis, and communications strategies to advance a cause.

Organizational and management issues important in delivering a service or program are likely to be narrow in scope. Most attention goes to budgeting and project management, the basic elements needed to ensure that the organization and program can function. Staff are recruited for their programmatic expertise and skills; organizational functions tend to be treated as marginal. The organization is little more than a convenient venue where programs are implemented.

Program Expansion Capacity

Once a nonprofit decides to expand its program delivery across multiple sites, or grow significantly at one site, it faces a different class of challenges that force it to devote more attention to questions of management and organization. As it grows, the organization must respond with more effort to issues it once handled informally in a small operation. Organizational issues can no longer fit on the back of an envelope. With more staff, funders, and sites, more formal systems are needed to handle payroll, financial control, promotion, and program documentation. Fundraising needs to be handled deliberately and strategically. Supervisory responsibilities are broader than just program implementation; nonprogrammatic staff will be needed. All of the program delivery capacities remain critical, but performance is now more dependent on organizational decisions and capacities as well.

Building either program delivery or program expansion capacity requires enormous effort. Appropriately, funders, nonprofits, researchers, and educators have devoted considerable resources to meeting these challenges. But regarding the third capacity which drives organizational effectiveness most directly, the conversation has barely begun.

Adaptive Capacity

This is the resource that an organization needs to be sure that it is delivering on its mission. It is one thing to deliver a program. It is another to ask and know whether the program is really relevant given the changing needs of clients and communities, or whether it is really *well-delivered* given the tendency of staff to burn out or allow quality to slip. It is yet another thing to know where and how to change programs and strategies so that the organization is delivering on its mission. For an organization to be more than the sum of its programs, it needs the ability to ask, listen, reflect, and *adapt*.[6]

Adaptive capacity can be built through a set of organizational processes, although these processes differ substantially from those involved in delivering a program, expanding the program, or even establishing financial stability. The processes of adaptive capacity support a different set of organizational goals, including:

- *Learning*: to measure performance and identify both problems and possibilities for improvements
- *Responsiveness*: to understand how well clients are served and what changes need to be made to improve the quality of service

21

Program Delivery	Program Expansion	Adaptive
The organization and program are almost synonymous: Most attention is on the knowledge needed to address a specific social problem or challenge.	The growth of an organization across sites requires more attention to organizational capacities.	To ensure that its programs are really advancing the organization's mission, an organization needs to continuously assess and improve its performance.
Key capacities:	*Key capacities:*	*Key capacities:*
Program knowledge about the nature of social problems and the solutions that are likely to work.	In addition to *program delivery* capacities:	In addition to *program delivery* and apart from *program expansion* capacities:
Project management: to organize the service delivery.	*Personnel:* standard policies to ensure equity across sites; better record-keeping to keep track of a larger staff's pay, benefits, and work histories.	*Innovativeness:* to develop new programs that will improve communities or the welfare of clients.
The critical basics to keep program going: budgeting, cash management.	*Financial control:* the question "How are we financially?" requires information about which sites or contracts are in good shape and where the trouble spots are.	*Responsiveness:* to ensure that programs are continuously modified to meet changing needs and seize new opportunities.
For *advocacy organizations*, critical capacities include research, analysis, and communications.	*Fundraising:* more strategic as organization needs to attract new funders.	*Motivation:* to attract, retain, and support the staff needed to deliver quality services and to keep the organization creative and effective.
	Training: to train new site managers and assure quality implementation across sites.	*Learning:* to develop and/or apply research on program efficacy and on organizational performance (e.g., by measuring performance with tools like benchmarking).
Performance—primarily a matter of program implementation efficacy and outcomes.	**Performance**—now a matter of organization and management as well as program expertise; new sites can be added and sustained only with more attention to functions above.	*Quality:* to ensure that, in addition to working (i.e., creating desired effect), service or program is delivered *well*.
		Collaboration: to ensure that community problems requiring the efforts of more than one nonprofit are served effectively (e.g., by convening, joint planning, assessing comparative value-added).
		Performance—enlarged to include not just program outcomes and organizational efficiency, but also organizational effectiveness and mission impact.

Exhibit 1–2 Organizational capacities.

- *Innovativeness*: to use the organization's people and knowledge to create new programs
- *Motivation*: to create jobs and organizations where staff and volunteers see the results of their work—the foundation for motivating people

These organizational processes enable a nonprofit to adapt its programs and practices so it can deliver on its mission. Fortunately, as the following chapters explain, these processes can be studied, learned, and tested by organizations willing to take on the challenge of improving performance.

WHY ADAPTIVE CAPACITY?

Why take on the challenge of performance when many nonprofits are not only, or even primarily, in the business of delivering service? As many nonprofit stakeholders point out, the nonprofit sector's *raison d'être* is not purely service delivery.[7] It also fosters social benefits that are vital to a democratic society, but that seem to have little to do with organizational performance. First, the nonprofit sector gives citizens a venue for self-expression, allowing individuals to act on deeply held beliefs and address pressing concerns. Second, the nonprofit sector is our arena for advocacy, through which citizens can highlight weaknesses in society and promote solutions, often bringing provocative and unsettling voices to the forefront. Third, the nonprofit sector is home to citizen associations through which people band together to work on common social goals. For some organizations, the "knitting together" from this associative activity, or the powerful changes in attitudes that can result, provides sufficient justification for their existence. So why should these nonprofits in pursuit of these goals worry about organizational performance?

If they do become focused on organizational capacity, won't they compromise distinctive nonprofit values? Would focusing on organizational capacity stifle innovation? Would "professionalization" substantially change the culture of organizations and have a dramatic effect on the way the sector is viewed? Would a focus on building organizational capacity lead to a preoccupation with market share and fundraising at the expense of the mission?

These hazards are the very reason organizations *should* develop their capacity for performance. Whether they deliver programs, act as advocates or associations, or some combination, virtually every nonprofit organization obligates itself to three groups of stakeholders: clients, employees, and funders. And organizational capacity—especially the adaptive capacity that links mission and outcomes—is a critical resource for doing right by these constituencies and honoring a nonprofit's values.

First, adaptive capacity enables organizations to create value for the clients or communities they serve. For direct service providers of housing, education, social services, or medical care, it is easy to see that the client or community deserves innovative, high-quality, responsive, effective services. Especially when a third party, like government or private donors, pays for services to their clients, nonprofits need to be very vigilant about quality. If their clients are not paying for the service, or choosing the service providers, they have little clout in demanding better quality. It is up to the organization to build the capacity for ensuring quality. Even citizen associations and advocacy organizations have constituencies. An association can let its membership down and advocates can fail to deliver for their causes by performing poorly. The processes of adaptive capacity—for learning, innovating, measuring, and improving performance—are all about creating value for these stakeholders.

Second, adaptive capacity enables organizations to motivate staff and volunteers. While we sometimes tend to romanticize them as citizen crusaders perpetually motivated by a social cause, we also have to grant that many of them are employees—people with jobs, if not careers and professions. Nonprofits owe their people a work environment where they can develop new skills, take on challenging assignments, and have the tools that enable them to succeed at those assignments. The organizational processes that support learning and motivation can help an organization deliver for its own people, so they can deliver for clients or communities.

Finally, adaptive capacity enables organizations to demonstrate their comparative value to funders, whether they be dues-paying members, government agencies, donors, or foundations. The fact that most organizations are stewards of other people's resources obligates them to deliver for those funders, by ensuring that their performance is of high quality. Adaptive capacity is not about getting more money—though it may lead to that—as much as it is about spending that money well and demonstrating comparative value, so that funders, staff, and clients are honored.

SIZE AND THE POWER OF PERFORMANCE

Even if these capacities are vital to all types of nonprofits, are they accessible to small organizations? It has often been assumed that smaller nonprofits cannot and need not, build the organizational capacity to perform well. Therefore, the commitment and determination of their staffs and boards will have to suffice. Considering the vital role small nonprofits play in meeting social needs, this cavalier attitude is risky. Not only do we entrust small nonprofits with important tasks like child care, inner-city housing development, services for the homeless, and youth development, but we have made a substantial public investment in them. According to the Independent Sector (the national association that encourages nonprofit initiative), excluding religious organizations, 41 percent of nonprofits had annual expenses of $100,000 or less.[8] And since many of these organizations have no desire to grow beyond their local community, they face the choice of building capacity at a small scale or they risk missing opportunities to create value.

In fact, even with limited resources, small nonprofits can build organizational capacity. The basic functions of bookkeeping and finance, for example, are essential to long-term survival. With lower-cost computers and user-friendly software, small nonprofits can handle these organizational challenges. Alternatively, some are relying on affiliations with larger nonprofits or with subcontractors to provide these functions.

Small organizations also need and can develop some of the fundamental assets of high performance: the adaptive capacity to support learning, responsiveness, innovativeness, and motivation. Even without expensive benchmarking consultants, many small nonprofits study the performance of other organizations and assess the implications for themselves. In fact, large businesses (and non-profits) often need high-end consulting approaches because their size makes it *harder* to turn their tankers around. Small nonprofits typically remain closer to their clients and donors, and can respond accordingly. Examples from our inquiry—of homeless-serving organizations, small health clinics, local social service agencies— underscore the value of management processes that help small non-profits perform well.

BUILDING AN AGENDA FOR ORGANIZATIONAL CAPACITY

Our inquiry into organizational capacity in the nonprofit sector has a larger agenda: looking not only at what individual organizations can accomplish, but also at expanding attention to performance in the nonprofit sector as a whole. Our goal is to stimulate discussion and work on a more *effective* nonprofit sector, not merely a more *efficient* one. To create that kind of sector, nonprofit organizations and stakeholders must build organizational capacity together, and not just leave individual managers and boards struggling in isolation.

The first step in building that support for more effective non-profits is to shift our thinking about what a nonprofit really needs to deliver on its mission. Current attitudes about organizational capacity are far too narrow to support investment in organizational performance. Most frequently, nonprofit funders tend to see any investment in organizations as overhead, deadweight costs that take money away from program beneficiaries. (This is the pervasive attitude that leads to annual report pie charts proudly depicting the smallest possible share of expenditures for overhead or administration.) Slightly more positive is the attitude that modest support for basic organizational systems, especially financial controls, is the necessary cost of efficiency and accountability. We need support for the proposition that organizational capacity, especially the adaptive capacity needed to deliver on a mission, is a much more vital resource for the nonprofit sector. Our current limited vision should concern not just nonprofit managers. All of us, especially the people served by nonprofits, will benefit from making organizational capacity a new priority for the nonprofit sector.

ADDITIONAL READING

Backer, Thomas E. *Dissemination Utilization Strategies for Foundations: Adding Value to Grantmaking*. Kansas City, MO: Ewing Marion Kauffman Foundation, 1995.

Bryson, John M. *Strategic Planning for Public and Private Nonprofit Organizations: A Guide to Strengthening and Sustaining Organizational Development*. San Francisco: Jossey-Bass, 1988.

Moss Kanter, Rosabeth. *The Change Masters: Innovation and Entrepreneurship in the American Corporation*. New York: Simon & Schuster, 1983.

Light, Paul. *Sustaining Innovation: Creating Nonprofit and Government Organizations That Innovate Naturally*. San Francisco: Jossey-Bass, 1998.

Morgan, Gareth. *Images of Organizations*. Thousand Oaks, CA: Sage Publications, 1997.

Senge, Peter M. *The Fifth Discipline*. New York: Currency Doubleday, 1990.

Schon, Donald A. *The Reflective Practitioner: How Professionals Think in Action*. London: Temple Smith, 1983.

Ulrich, David and Dale Lake. *Organizational Capability: Competing from the Inside Out*. New York : John Wiley & Sons, 1990.

Ulvin, Peter and David Miller. "Paths to Scaling-up: Alternative Strategies for Local Nongovernmental Organizations," *Human Organization*, Vol. 55, No. 3, 1996.

ENDNOTES

[1]Michael Edwards and David Hulme, eds., *Making a Difference: NGOs and Development in a Changing World* (London: Earthscan Publications Ltd, 1992). Their going-to-scale schema uses the terms "additive," "diffusive," and "multiplicative" where we use "expansion," "diffusion," and "policy reform," respectively.

27

[2]See Thomas E. Backer, *Dissemination Utilization Strategies for Foundations: Adding Value to Grantmaking* (Kansas City, MO: Ewing Marion Kauffman Foundation, 1995).

[3]For more on this distinction, see Paul C. Light, *Sustaining Innovation: Creating Nonprofit and Government Organizations That Innovate Naturally* (San Francisco: Jossey-Bass, 1998).

[4]Sara Mosle, "The Stealth Chancellor," *New York Times Sunday Magazine*, August 15, 1997.

[5]Thanks to Professor Mark H. Moore of the Kennedy School of Government at Harvard for help in distinguishing these capacities.

[6]For a discussion of adaptive capacity in a leadership context, see Ronald A. Heifetz, *Leadership Without Easy Answers* (Cambridge, MA: The Belknap Press of Harvard University, 1994).

[7]For a discussion of the roles played by nonprofit organizations, see Lester M. Salamon, *Holding the Center: America's Nonprofit Sector at the Crossroads* (New York: the Nathan Cummings Foundation, 1997).

[8]However, these organizations control just 2 percent of the total assets in the sector, and receive less than 3 percent of the total public support. Independent Sector, *The Nonprofit Almanac* (San Francisco: Jossey-Bass, 1996).

CHAPTER TWO

Cross-Sector Lessons on Organizational Capacity

FRAMING QUESTIONS

▶ Why build organizational capacity when there are such pressing social problems?

▶ How does organizational capacity differ in the for-profit and nonprofit sectors?

▶ What would a focus on performance mean for individual organizations, and for the nonprofit sector as a whole?

▶ Does building organizational capacity compromise a nonprofit's values and mission?

As we explain in our introduction,[1] we took a cross-sector approach to our inquiry—comparing nonprofits and for-profits—for two reasons. First, businesses have developed a substantial body of information and experience on organizational capacity building, which could provide lessons and best practices. Second, the for-profit experience provides a backdrop against which to see the distinctive assets and liabilities of nonprofits. From there, the cross-sector comparison allows us to explore the possibility of "cultural adaptation"—extracting ideas and processes from one environment for testing and application in another. Our goal throughout was to study how organizational methods, either from the for-profit or nonprofit sector, could support the social agenda, values, and missions of nonprofit organizations.

Our cross-sector analysis proved particularly powerful in illuminating how the for-profit and nonprofit sectors see the potential of organizational capacity. It showed, in brief, that *for-profit managers are not inherently better managers; they are better-supported managers.* We found that managers in both sectors use many of the same or similar practices to advance the fundamental goals of their respective organizations. But nonprofit managers face additional challenges coming both from within their organizations and the external operating environment, making their work considerably harder. Nonprofit managers are forced to manage upstream, as it were, against the conventions, attitudes, and behaviors of their sector. These dynamics should trouble anyone who believes that smart, well-managed organizations are critical to advancing social missions.

> *For-profit managers are not inherently better managers; they are* better-supported *managers.*

Our inquiry generated three key findings that describe the scope and implications of the challenge.

EXCELLENT MANAGEMENT PRACTICES ARE IMPORTANT: THEY HELP ADVANCE AN ORGANIZATION'S MISSION IN BOTH SECTORS

We found that both nonprofit and for-profit managers use similar management practices for the same reasons: to get the results they care most about. Businesses consistently explained how their use of organizational tools helped them earn more profits by improving their products and services. Nonprofits consistently explained how they used the same tools, or close equivalents, to generate social impacts. In other words, they value organizational capacity because it helps them deliver on a mission.

For example, the international relief and development organization CARE uses a sophisticated form of benchmarking in much the same way as Xerox, the company credited with exploiting benchmarking most aggressively and creatively. At CARE, a benchmarking process led directly to the creation of more effective water projects. As a result, more people in more places enjoy better health.

At the Vera Institute of Justice, the program-development process conforms closely to the cutting-edge model created by product-development specialists at Arthur D. Little, the consulting giant that serves many world-class companies. Vera's method for developing a new immigrant-screening process helped the Immigration and Naturalization Service make more efficient use of limited detention space. More importantly, it did so in a way that allowed for a more humane and just detention policy, directly advancing Vera's mission through tangible reforms.

THE MARKETPLACE SUPPORTS THE ORGANIZATIONAL CAPACITY OF BUSINESSES—THE NONPROFIT ENVIRONMENT STARVES IT

Two different stories emerged from the two sectors on the question of what enables managers to perform. The business managers described an environment that supports their organization-building efforts. The nonprofit leaders described an indifferent, sometimes hostile environment that can undermine their efforts to build strong organizations.[2]

In the for-profit sector, organizational capacity is valued as the *primary* means for succeeding in the marketplace. Investors, corporate boards, CEOs, and managers all understand that success comes not from a product or service alone, but from an organization's ability to market, distribute, and improve it. Understanding that organizations and products together create success leads to investment in the processes that build organizational performance. Business schools, consulting firms, and an expanding body of research all reinforce the value of organizational capacity and encourage leaders to take it seriously.

The relationship between programs and organizational capacity is strikingly different in the nonprofit sector. The two are considered almost as competitors in a zero-sum struggle for limited resources. Money invested in organizations is considered lost to direct service. While managers might know their organizations need certain capacities to be effective, funding guidelines, charity watchdog groups, individual donors, and the vast weight of popular opinion all send a very different message: Don't spend on organizations. So while for-profit managers are awash in training, research, and education, and boards and investors encourage them to take organizational capacity seriously, nonprofit managers are expected to get heroic results out of their organizations with few of these supports.

> *In the nonprofit world, programs and organizational capacity are almost seen as competitors in a zero-sum struggle for limited resources.*

Unfortunately, the low overhead so esteemed in the nonprofit sector can signal not only frugality but also low performance. A 1994 review of Rwandan refugee assistance suggests that the lowest-overhead operators in Rwanda apparently were not as effective as their bigger, more expensive counterparts.[3] Some of the frugal organizations sent off-the-shelf rehydrating fluids—cheap, but useless for the particular health problems of the Rwandans. They sent personally committed volunteer doctors, flown in and out at great cost, who were not on the ground long enough to get oriented and proficient. What looked like fat in the bigger organizations with more overhead and headquarters staff actually was muscle that helped them react quickly and effectively.

From a distance, the difference between building an organization's capacity for success (muscle) and assembling a self-serving empire (fat) remains hard to distinguish. More money for planning, market research, or quality control may mean better results or it may just mean more staff and bigger organizations, a potential outcome that makes funders wary of investing in organizations. Usually, the scarcity of resources in the nonprofit sector makes it safer to put more into "direct service" than into organizational capacity. Unfortunately, what is safer is not always smarter.

This is not to say that organizational capacity will not help nonprofits attract more funds. The relationship between organizational capacity and funding prospects—Does it pay?—has been difficult to assess. But a recent study by Joseph Galaskiewicz and Wolfgang Bielefeld of Minneapolis–St. Paul nonprofits (using data from 1980 to 1994) found that efficient, rational, and customer-oriented organizations (both large and small) can better compete and grow. Their comprehensive study found that even those organizations operating outside market-like environments benefited from these strategies, increasing their donated income and volunteers.[4] While this study suggests that organizational capacity seems to attract funds, it does not necessarily follow that funders actively seek out, support, and reward it. They might like the results but not care about the methods that generated them, which is consistent with the final theme to emerge in our inquiry.

INDIFFERENCE TO ORGANIZATIONAL CAPACITY HAS ITS ROOTS DEEP IN THE NONPROFIT CULTURE OF SERVICE

Why is there indifference to how organizations excel and what they need in order to perform well? Our discussions with nonprofit managers suggest that organizational issues hold little appeal for the several types of nonprofit employees who populate much of the sector.

With a commitment to serving those in need, and with few resources to do it, many nonprofit employees develop a "just do it" attitude that places more value on service than on the analysis and measurement needed to improve organizational performance. In this environment, organizational development may seem not only uninteresting, but like an indulgence that will deprive clients or beneficiaries of resources. Many nonprofit workers, moreover, believe in what one called "the artistry" of their work. They tend to see their efforts as the product of personal commitment, perhaps professional training, and personal experience. They feel that measuring their efforts with the tools of organizational performance diminishes this artistry. Moreover, many would see such analysis as inherently competitive and punitive, designed to uncover suboptimal performance and thereby threaten the cooperative nature of nonprofit workplaces.

Within the service-oriented front-line ranks are two slightly different profiles: professionals and social entrepreneurs. Professionals, in fields like social work, public health, or education, are obviously not content with service alone; they believe their specialized training will help them achieve results. Social entrepreneurs, similarly, are inspired to develop an innovative idea, convert it into a program or service, mobilize supporters and funders, and bring their personal passions to the job of getting it implemented. But as a number of nonprofit managers in our roundtables suggested, the very people attracted to service, the professions, or entrepreneurship are often the ones most reluctant to engage in the analysis and comparison often needed to improve *organizational* performance.

While we do and should value professionals who respond to a service calling, we need to think about how to equip these committed professionals to succeed as managers and leaders of organizations. And the entrepreneur who creates a new program cannot run on commitment alone if the program requires an organization to implement and sustain it over time. Service and performance should go hand-in-hand in these cases, but the nonprofit culture speaks mostly to service.

Added to the service-orientation and culture of many employees is the funding system, which also tends to marginalize the issue of organizational performance. The third-party payer system prevalent in much of the nonprofit sector reinforces the service culture. Government contracts tend to reward previously proven methods, not innovations. Funders want to back successful programs (and often won't signal dissatisfaction as long as the money is "well spent" and accounted for). Clients (who don't pay and often don't have alternatives) can't signal the need for change. Instead of leading, or trying to better their previous efforts, many organizations get drawn into simply providing.

As the many examples uncovered in our inquiry suggest, this culture is not an inescapable trap. Organizations can preserve the values of their staff while adapting organizational tools that can help them assess and enhance their performance.

BUILDING ADAPTIVE CAPACITY FOR HIGH PERFORMANCE

Developing organizational capacity is slow, difficult work even in the most receptive of cultures. In the nonprofit world in particular, it requires more than just a clever plan and a fistful of resources. Creating a high-performing nonprofit requires lots of attention to the "guts" of an organization, getting to know how things work (or don't work) now, and how they might operate more effectively. It takes a lot of tinkering with the gears and levers that turn energy into outcomes. It demands an understanding of specific organizational practices and how they fit into the larger mission. It teaches the patience needed for creating incremental change.

In the chapters that follow, we offer an overview of management processes that support organizational capacity. Any of them offer a valid starting point for organizational capacity building. Working in concert, they can provide the basis for lasting change—both within organizations and in society at large, through the more effective fulfillment of a social mission.

ADDITIONAL READING

Collins, James C. and Jerry I. Porras. *Built to Last: Successful Habits of Visionary Companies*. New York: Harper Collins, 1994.

Drucker, Peter M. *Crossover Between Nonprofit and Business Sectors* (symposium report). Tokyo: Sasakawa Peace Foundation, 1994.

Kotter, John P. and James L. Heskett. *Corporate Culture and Performance*. New York: Macmillan, 1992.

Lorsch, Jay. "Managing Culture: Invisible Barriers to Strategic Change," *California Management Review*, Vol. XXVIII, No. 2, Winter, 1986.

Schein, Edgar H. *Organizational Culture and Leadership*. San Francisco: Jossey-Bass, 1992.

ENDNOTES

[1]See "A Cross-Sector Look at Performance" on page 4.

[2]For example, as Lisbeth B. Schorr writes in *Common Purpose*: "In the private sector, the context is the market, and profit the measure of success. Rules and regulations may intrude, but they stop short of prescribing the very essence of what the enterprise does and how it does it. By contrast, human services, education, and community building are shaped by highly complex systems that specify what you may or may not do." (New York: Anchor Books/Doubleday, 1997, pp. 29–30.)

[3]Raymond Bonner, "Post-Mortem for Charities: Compassion Wasn't Enough in Rwanda," *New York Times*, December 18, 1994.

[4]Joseph Galaskiewicz and Wolfgang Bielefeld, *Nonprofit Organizations in an Age of Uncertainty: A Study of Organizational Change* (Forthcoming, Aldine de Gruyter).

PART II

Building the Organizational Capacity That Leads to High Performance

CHAPTER 3

Quality Processes: Advancing Mission by Meeting Client Needs

FRAMING QUESTIONS

▶ Are we staying in touch with local needs as we grow and diversify?

▶ Is today's program simply responding to yesterday's problem?

▶ How can we measure quality?

To most nonprofits, instituting formal systems for quality service and client responsiveness is a coals-to-Newcastle proposition: Almost every nonprofit was founded explicitly to respond to a community need—with quality services or resources. Indeed, most nonprofits continue to evolve over time in response to changing needs. They frequently ask: Do our programs respond to the needs of our community? Are we implementing them well? Are our staff welcoming, respectful, accessible, supportive? For most nonprofits, the biggest challenge in ensuring responsiveness and quality service is not *commitment* but rather *capacity*. They may lack the tools and resources that will help them assess client needs and preferences and, more importantly, implement changes that will improve their quality and responsiveness.

Quality processes translate commitment to quality into results by helping organizations: (1) determine whether and how a program is satisfying clients, (2) measure the performance of management and staff, and (3) identify practical ways to improve services. Quality processes complement the information that most businesses and nonprofits already collect through bottom-line figures and program evaluation, but illuminate different aspects of performance. Both the bottom line and evaluations provide important snapshots that can tell how viable an organization or program is. Quality processes are different in that they provide continuous feedback about performance, help organizations figure out where to make improvements, and keep the focus on the customers or clients that the organization intends to serve.

> *Quality processes help organizations figure out* why *they are succeeding and* how *they can sustain or improve customer satisfaction.*

As the profiles in this chapter show, quality processes give organizations the capacity to deliver on their commitment to excellence and responsiveness. In two of the cases—the Ritz-Carlton Hotel Company, a leader in the luxury hotel market, and AVSC International, an international public health nonprofit—quality systems focus on improving the delivery of a service. In the third case—Wellspring House, a much younger, smaller nonprofit—a commitment to quality and responsiveness has been built into processes they use to design programs and set strategies. Across sectors, program areas, and size, these organizations have developed tools that support organizational responsiveness.

RITZ-CARLTON HOTEL COMPANY

Ritz-Carlton hotels have earned a reputation for quality service. Facing a glut of hospitality providers when they entered the business in 1983, the company's founders decided to claim the "top 5 percent of the luxury traveling marketplace." As Darrell Ross, quality leader for Ritz-Carlton explained, extensive market research helped the company determine that a quality strategy could differentiate their product from competitors'. It was "the customer's idea," says Ross, for Ritz-Carlton to commit "to the highest levels of personal service and uncompromising levels of cleanliness."

This strategy has fundamentally shaped organizational practices at Ritz-Carlton, requiring a "total resource commitment" to quality, with all practices and personnel aligned to support service goals. Choosing the right properties, creating appealing design features, and offering a broad range of guest amenities were only the starting points. To succeed, Ritz-Carlton needed every guest experience, each one shaped by the actions and decisions of employees throughout the organization, to meet or surpass the highest expectations. Meeting this universal quality standard meant, in turn, developing a distinctive culture and an array of practices, tools, and incentives to support all employees in their efforts.

All of these approaches reinforce the fundamental mission of Ritz-Carlton: guest-defined quality. The process begins with hiring, where recruiters look for employees who show enthusiasm for the highest levels of personal service. The service commitment is constantly reinforced through all levels of the organization. Ritz-Carlton President and COO, Horst Schulze, personally leads training and orientations for employees at new hotels.

After hiring, the quality-service vision is reinforced continuously. All employees carry a "credo card" that embeds the quality strategy in a code of behavior. (See Exhibit 3-1.) All front-line personnel focus on a "behavior of the week" in an effort to promote understanding of and commitment to quality practices. Managers regularly recognize employees throughout the organization for their quality service by awarding bonuses, often in the form of free meals or stays at one of the hotels.

For those who will not or cannot live up to the commitment, dismissal is a possibility. But Ross maintains that the unconverted are not attracted to Ritz-Carlton in the first place, and would leave on their own in short order because the company has created an "atmosphere where mediocrity is not tolerated." And expectations are high in the Ritz-Carlton culture. For example, Ross explained, if

---

- The Ritz-Carlton Hotel is a place where the genuine care and comfort of our guests is our highest mission.
- We pledge to provide the finest personal service and facilities for our guests, who will always enjoy a warm, relaxed yet refined ambiance.
- The Ritz-Carlton Hotel experience enlivens the senses, instills well-being, and fulfills even the unexpressed wishes and needs of our guests.

Exhibit 3-1   The Ritz-Carlton Quality Credo.

a maintenance worker changing a light bulb in a hallway sees a guest carrying an ice bucket, it becomes the maintenance worker's job to take the bucket, fill it, and deliver it to the guest's room. As the company's service materials explain: Any employee who receives a customer complaint owns the complaint.

Ritz-Carlton does not rely on culture alone to produce results. It has developed tools and policies that help employees meet high expectations. For example, the company makes extensive use of technology to track the preferences of frequent guests. Quality departments at each hotel help managers and front-line staff analyze service quality, study service problems, and develop strategies for improvement. Quality leaders also help different departments coordinate their efforts to ensure better results. Perhaps most important, front-line staff are given authority to make decisions on the spot, before it's too late to resolve a guest's problem. Many front-line employees are authorized to spend up to $2,000 without approval to keep a guest satisfied. If a room is not ready at the promised hour, for example, a staff member can offer a guest a complimentary meal or business work space to ease the delay.

> *Front-line staff have the authority to make decisions on the spot, before it's too late to resolve a guest's problem.*

Ross emphasizes that empowering staff to meet expectations is fundamental to the quality strategy: "By driving employee satisfaction, you drive guest satisfaction and guest retention for long-term profitability." In addition to discretion and the coaching from quality leaders, employees are encouraged to use the company's formal quality network to propose ideas that would improve performance, guest satisfaction and, not least, the work environment itself.

The quality strategy has paid off for Ritz-Carlton, which has held its place in the top end of the market. The quality systems that led to this approach are widely praised and discussed in the business literature. In 1997, the company was awarded the coveted U.S. Department of Commerce's Malcolm Baldridge National Quality Award.

AVSC INTERNATIONAL

AVSC International,[1] a 55-year-old nonprofit organization, provides technical and financial assistance to operators of family planning and reproductive health services. AVSC works with direct-service providers and with intermediaries—including universities, ministries of health, and nongovernmental organizations (NGOs) in over 29 countries (mostly in developing countries, but in the United States as well). Most of the clients served by these organizations are nonpaying.

AVSC International developed COPE (for Client-Oriented, Provider-Efficient) as a quality tool for service providers in 1989.[2] As Dr. Pamela Lynam, senior advisor for Quality of Care, explains, AVSC wanted to help providers move from a vague commitment to quality to operational strategies that lead to results. "We wanted to find a way to make quality real. We're talking about quality all the time but sometimes it's difficult for people to actually concretely imagine what we're talking about."

The COPE process, a practical, inexpensive method, allowed cash-strapped, overburdened health providers, often working in harsh conditions, to assess and improve the quality of their service delivery. Conceived in collaboration with the Ministry of Health and several NGOs in Kenya and Nigeria, COPE guides organizations through a four-step process over a two-day period. Initially facilitated by AVSC staff during a regular field visit, the process is subsequently led by local supervisors.

43

The first step is a self-assessment by local staff. AVSC does not play the role of the "quality enforcer" who arrives to detect and sanction lapses. Instead, AVSC works with the site and supervisors, at their request, to engage the entire staff in an assessment of their efforts. AVSC begins by facilitating a series of short introductory sessions where the staff, in groups of about ten, discuss quality in a very practical way. They begin to reflect on some of the problems that clients may encounter in their services. Cynthia Steele, director of Special Programs, explains, "The important thing about the COPE process is that it's owned by the people who do it. This is something for their use, to help themselves. It uses the wisdom of the experts—the people who work in that clinic and the people who use those services."

> *"The COPE process is owned by the people who do it. This is something for their use, to help themselves."*

The second element, the client flow analysis, was modeled on a tool developed by the U.S. Centers for Disease Control in response to one of the perennial service problems of health clinics: waiting time. Some providers have become so inured to the problem that they actually rationalize long wait times as a benefit for patients, claiming clients value the informal contact of the waiting room as quality social time. The idea that clients enjoy the chance to "have a good chat with their neighbors is absolutely ridiculous," says Lynam. "People don't like waiting around for health services anywhere in the world."

To understand where delays occur, clients receive a slip of paper as they enter the clinic. Every time a clinic employee interacts with a client—for example, at check-in, in an initial interview, or at discharge—she or he records the time and initials the patient's slip. At the end of the visit, the client leaves behind the slip, which now carries a record of how the client moved through the clinic and where delays occurred. These slips are collected, and the resulting data summarized in graphs that allow the staff to see trends, focus on particular features of wait times, and develop potential remedies.

Clinic staff carry out the third part of the COPE process, client interviews, over the two-day assessment period. Using a short list of questions developed by AVSC, they elicit feedback on client satisfaction by asking, for example: "Did you get what you wanted when you came here today? How did people treat you? Do you have any suggestions about how we might improve our services?" The clinic employees themselves are the interviewers, and fit these interviews in as they go about their work. Client responses are sorted and summarized to provide another means of assessment.

Staff handle the fourth component, development of an action plan, at the end of the two-day visit. They reconvene to review the results of the self-assessment, flow analysis, and client interviews, and develop a plan of action. They identify problems, solutions, and persons responsible for follow-up, and establish timetables. Although some of the problems identified are beyond the influence of the staff, typically they uncover a number of improvements possible within their own resources. Work processes can often be adjusted to reduce waiting times. Many clinics find ways to become more user-friendly. For example, some are located deep within the labyrinth of large hospitals, forcing clients who want privacy to repeatedly ask for directions; better signage corrects this problem in a simple way.

Most organizations that try COPE use it repeatedly, sometimes as often as every six months, although AVSC is quick to admit some organizations use it once, then never again. Based on its experience in 29 countries, AVSC continues to adapt and improve the tool. According to Lynam, one of the biggest challenges is to keep the system simple. Suggestions to add "fish-bone diagrams" and other familiar tools of more sophisticated quality systems have been rejected. For a more in-depth search for the cause of a problem, AVSC suggests simple, yet effective, techniques such as asking "Why?" several times to probe the underlying reasons for problems identified.

In reassessing the impact of COPE, AVSC has found impressive results in clinic problems solved and numbers of staff energized (see Exhibit 3-2). Providers, AVSC says, claim COPE "increased

Total number of problems identified	65
Total number solvable	50
Total number solved	38
Percentage solved of total	58%
Percentage solved of solvable	76%

Exhibit 3-2   Findings from a typical COPE project.

motivation, encouraged cooperation, made communication between different levels much easier, and increased sensitivity to
client needs." COPE has provided the structure for creating change.
As Lynam put it, "This terrible word 'empowering' really means
something. [Clinic staff] start to say, 'We can do that. Now let's
tackle this other thing which is bigger.'"

WELLSPRING HOUSE

*We basically gave up our jobs to share a home with others who needed a
home for awhile. We had a sense of wanting to practice quality hospitality
for people who simply didn't have homes. And it was very important for us
that the place be beautiful and that the structures that we put into place
together would be an embodiment of a community of teamwork.*

Nancy Schwoyer
Executive Director, Wellspring House

A commitment to quality was the cornerstone of what has
become Wellspring House, a nonprofit organization dedicated to
relieving and preventing homelessness in Gloucester, Massachusetts. As it evolved from a loose association of a few committed
individuals in 1980 to a growing organization tackling complex
social problems, Wellspring's systems for responsiveness evolved
as well. Unlike Ritz-Carlton and AVSC, whose quality systems
focus on service delivery, Wellspring used a quality and responsiveness approach to shape the planning and strategy development
that leads to service delivery.

Two years after "the crisis of homelessness found us," as
Schwoyer puts it, she and her colleagues began expanding their

network and establishing an organization that could serve larger numbers of people, including families. By 1988, Wellspring had expanded its reach beyond temporary relief and shelter for the homeless. It had bought, rehabilitated, and was managing three residential properties and had spun off a separate corporation to pursue affordable housing development.

As it grew, Wellspring moved from implicit personal commitment to conscious organizational strategies for sustaining responsiveness. Inclusivity was a central value from the outset; clients and a diverse cross-section of the community were always represented on the board. The staff were also influenced by Brazilian educator and social critic Paulo Freire's[3] "praxis" model for engaging disenfranchised people in an assessment of the social conditions that led to their problems. In the praxis model, poor people are not just consumers offering input to service providers, but citizens deciding on the most appropriate strategies for addressing social problems. Homelessness, for example, is seen as a symptom of deeper social and economic conditions whose solutions require more than just shelter.

Commenting on their practice of these principles, Schwoyer explained: "It's part of our culture to constantly reflect on what we are doing and to analyze the causes of the situations. What is it that causes poverty in our culture? Is our response appropriate to what is really going on here? So it has meant over the years being willing to be quite flexible to change."

With the number of its constituents and the scope of its services growing, Wellspring decided to take advantage of strategic planning services offered by the Boston Foundation's Fund for the Homeless, leading to a process that would help it operationalize the praxis principles and keep the organization responsive. The organization engaged homeless people, staff, board members, and community volunteers in an extensive self-assessment and strategic planning process. This particular planning model worked so well that the organization has repeated it four times since 1988.

In 1990, on the occasion of its tenth anniversary, Wellspring embarked on an ambitious and comprehensive assessment of the progress they and the community had made on homelessness, and toward an understanding of where to focus in the future. Using disciplined data-gathering, analysis and convening on a regular schedule, the Wellspring process not only empowered the clients themselves to be an important part of the problem-solving, but created a safe forum through which members of the community could sign up to help solve seemingly intractable problems. Community volunteers, for example, received training on how to interview former and current homeless people as part of the information collection.

The results of this research, published in 1991, became the occasion for convening a symposium of a cross-section of people from the entire community. Action groups were formed around the issues, including education, jobs, freedom from domestic violence, and safe neighborhoods. The action plans produced by the groups called for up to $1 million in resources. After a feasibility study, the Wellspring board committed to leading a campaign to raise the funds over a three-year period. It met its goal, and began implementing the projects, ahead of schedule.

DELIVERING ON MISSION WITH DISCIPLINED INFORMATION ANALYSIS

Ultimately, organizations take on the challenge of developing quality processes because they believe quality service is an essential part of their mission. If they regarded quality service merely as an amenity or a philosophical orientation, they would hardly trouble with the disciplined collection and analysis of data that are at the heart of any quality process.

> *It is precisely this detailed, methodical analysis that enables organizations to convert their commitment to quality into results that advance their mission.*

Both Ritz-Carlton and AVSC illustrate how an organization can approach quality as an essential part of its mission. The connection is simple at Ritz-Carlton: Quality is the cornerstone of the company's competitive strategy. Quality processes help the company achieve profitability. Through AVSC, the COPE process also helps organizations advance their missions. Although the clinics using COPE are in the day-to-day business of providing health services, the mission of many of these organizations extends further. They seek to share knowledge that will influence personal behavior and in turn improve people's health; or to improve the status of and opportunities for women; or to engender a sense of ownership and responsibility for personal, family, and community health. The quality of services directly affects these objectives. Unresponsive, inaccessible, or unwelcoming health services may be an insurmountable barrier to achieving these goals. Once people are alienated or discouraged from dealing with health institutions, the potential for educating and empowering them may be lost.

Because they see quality as an important dimension of their missions, all three of the organizations profiled were willing to develop the disciplined procedures needed to collect and assess information about client satisfaction. At Ritz-Carlton, staff throughout the organization collect an enormous amount of data through client surveys, critical-incident reports that analyze service failures, and market research about travelers' needs and preferences. Wellspring's planning process also featured systematic information-gathering, by training volunteers to use an interview protocol to solicit the community, particularly the homeless and formerly homeless, for ideas and input.

AVSC's COPE process is particularly disciplined. It differs, as one observer put it, from the widespread practice of discussing quality aspirations and problems in vague generalities at staff retreats "where everybody takes the day off and moans and groans, and nothing happens." The power of COPE arises from providing a structured process and analytical tools that uncover quality problems and lead to specific ideas for correcting them. "It's not by accident," remarks one observer of COPE, that many nonprofits "have never been able to talk concretely about quality. They've never had the language or the data."

To get the data that supports quality, these organizations must look beyond traditional measures of feedback. Like any business, Ritz-Carlton can use its bottom-line as a vital measure of performance. But bottom line figures provide little if any information about where and how to make improvements that can enhance profitability. The bottom line does not show which services customers value, how to develop new services that respond to their needs, or where to make improvements in existing services. For nonprofits, program evaluations provide similar information, with similar limitations. They usually speak to outcomes—whether a program works—and not to the processes that supported those outcomes. Their findings can help a nonprofit decide whether a program should be continued, discontinued, or expanded. But they are usually less useful in helping nonprofits understand how and where they could change its processes and procedures to improve quality.

Without this finer-grained information about quality, many nonprofits risk becoming isolated from the clients and communities they set out to serve. Most are used to responding to funders, but how many see clients as consumers who have both choice and voice? When third parties, not clients themselves, pay for services, and when clients have few or no choices about where to seek a service, market-like feedback systems cannot signal low satisfaction levels. As our exploration of benchmarking also suggests (see Chapter 5), the only alternative is to deliberately collect feedback from constituents and determine how to adapt services and operations to respond to their needs. Once organizations understand that they can use a disciplined quality process to advance their mission and ensure responsiveness, they are more likely to obligate themselves to their clients by taking on this difficult work.

> *Most nonprofits respond to funders, but how many see clients as consumers who have both choice and voice?*

Quality Processes Create More Work for Staff, but Give Them Better Tools to Succeed

A wary staff can quickly undermine a quality process, and managers need to carefully consider how to develop staff support for this work. There are several risks. A good quality process is likely to mean additional work for nearly everyone in the organization, not just a pet project for a quality enthusiast. Quality processes, moreover, force people to uncover and assess performance weaknesses, a potentially demoralizing activity. But as the cases profiled here show, an effective quality process can actually empower staff: It demands more of staff, but also gives them the tools to accomplish more. And accomplishing more leads inevitably to motivation and job satisfaction.

Quality processes almost always require staff throughout the organization to participate. A "quality department" working on its own is not enough. Ritz-Carlton hotels have designated "quality leaders," but their role is to sustain what the company calls a "total resource commitment" to quality. The quality leaders help managers and front-line staff assess and improve all aspects of service. Similarly, AVSC plays the role of quality-facilitator, while local staff conduct the assessment of their own performance. Lynam points out that a clinic's medical staff, administrators, secretaries, and maintenance staff are all typically involved in assessing quality and developing improvement strategies.

Inspiring already overburdened staff to take on any additional work is difficult, but the nature of quality processes only compounds the challenge. Because of its focus on detecting and correcting weaknesses, a quality process can easily discourage staff. They may hear "You're not good enough," when quality processes are really asking "How can we become better?" Reflecting on her experience in a Catholic religious order before forming Wellspring, Nancy Schwoyer noted this tendency. Some in the order felt that if church leadership was "calling on us to renew, you're calling us to do more, or do different. You're devaluing what we have been doing in the past." This risk of devaluing is inherent in quality processes. Lyman and Steele of AVSC report that when one NGO did use COPE findings in a "punitive way," it destroyed the value of the process by making staff defensive.

Effective quality processes will minimize the risk of resistance by structuring quality improvement as a collective project. A top-down, command-and-control approach to quality improvement is unlikely to work at many nonprofits, where staff commonly value collaboration. Even if a manager were inclined to try it, a top-down approach would have slim chances of success. Staff are unlikely to eagerly implement quality improvements if they have not participated up front in the diagnosis of the problems.

COPE establishes this type of up-front and widespread buy-in by involving the entire organization in discussions about potential quality problems. The entire staff is involved both in collecting data and proposing solutions. COPE also reduces the risk of defensiveness and demoralization by focusing not on individual performance, but on "how the system behaves as a whole. They don't end up focusing on a subset of providers who might have done worse than others. What they do is look at the overall patterns and say 'How can we all work better?' And it's usually not an individual problem but a system problem." Similarly, although the Ritz-Carlton will sanction employees for compromising quality standards, Ross emphasizes that it is the culture of the organization, created and sustained by all employees, that drives quality service.

Although the work in these quality processes is collective, it does not necessarily involve reorganizing the staff into formal teams. Unlike many of the most popular quality programs that swept through the business world 15 years ago, these efforts do not treat teams as if they were an end in themselves. For example, the organizations using COPE are not structured into teams, but they do experience the power of thinking and problem-solving together. Their joint work in creating solutions together and committing to action with each other may ultimately be more effective than the designation of teams.

Staff are also more willing to commit to the added work of a quality process if it empowers them by providing the tools, information, and authority they need to get results. A staff that constantly seeks out quality problems or opportunities but has no authority to follow up on them is sure to become demoralized, not to mention that the problems themselves will go uncorrected. At Ritz-Carlton, employees are equipped not just to detect problems but to resolve them as fast as possible. The best example is the company's policy authorizing front-line employees to make on-the-spot expenditures to solve a customer's problem. Similarly, in the organizations using COPE, the quality process focuses on identifying and following up on *attainable* improvements. An effective quality process provides both diagnosis and remedies—allowing staff to experience the satisfaction of solving problems.

At first glance, it may seem there can be nothing new about employee empowerment for most nonprofits. With their traditional preference for participatory decision making and a common dedication to the empowerment of disenfranchised constituents, many nonprofits are presumably full of empowered workers. In reality, however, the dedication of some employees is so strong that they tolerate working conditions and organizational practices that actually undermine their ability to serve people effectively. Most are aware of the hardships that commonly come with nonprofit work: low salary, trying work environments, even organizational instability. But when they accept these conditions with more resignation than indignation, employees are ill-equipped to meet the challenge of improving conditions for others. Quality processes that help employees translate a commitment to quality service into real results end up empowering and motivating staff.

Even as they support teamwork and empowerment in developing a process, managers will need tenacity and a willingness to make the staff and structural changes that are often needed for effectiveness. They need to remember that no one will move toward a different future unless it appears brighter and the way there is clear. Connecting quality and mission, and equipping staff to translate that connection into results, are essential to effective quality processes.

Quality Processes in Planning and Program Development

With their stress on disciplined data analysis and management strategy, quality processes may seem like evidence of the "bureaucratization" that so many nonprofits see as a threat to their social values and commitment. But when the underlying principles of quality processes are used to guide a nonprofit's planning and program development, the exact opposite is true: Quality processes protect against bureaucratization.

> *By keeping quality and responsiveness front-and-center, a nonprofit can ensure that it remains a community resource, not just a service provider interested in its own growth or sustainability.*

Wellspring provides an excellent case of quality and responsiveness in program planning and development. To grassroots community organizations, the experience and activities of Wellspring may not seem unusual. Wellspring's role as a community convenor is a familiar one for many community-based organizations. This type of associative behavior, where citizens band together informally to address a problem, is often a normal part of the "organizing" phase of nonprofit development. But as associations grow into formal organizations, service-delivery requirements and the imperatives of fundraising often lead them to focus as much on sustaining the institution as on serving the community. It is difficult to remain profoundly responsive to the community in the face of service-delivery demands.

Wellspring tenaciously maintained its commitment to solving the problems of the clients with responsive, high quality services. It eventually brought an entire community into its work, at exactly the point when the pressures of service-delivery expansion can lead nonprofits to focus less on their constituencies. Wellspring could well have become a professional organization that did not rely on its community to solve problems. As operations moved out of the founders' homes and into larger facilities addressing new needs, and as the state began funding those operations, the original notion of people answering a service calling by helping their neighbors could have been lost. Instead, Wellspring's systematic attention to client needs enabled it to grow while remaining responsive.

CONCLUSION

None of these organizations would argue that they discovered a new cure or drastically reduced the need for a set of services. But Ritz-Carlton, AVSC, and Wellspring demonstrate the possibilities for changing paradigms within organizations and even in communities and industries. In each case, quality systems and processes specifically designed to respond to the clients allowed organizations to lead as well as to serve. All of them intend to continue to use data analysis, client feedback, and staff involvement as they face the challenges of a changing environment.

ORGANIZATION PROFILES

The Ritz-Carlton Hotel Company, L.L.C.

3414 Peachtree Road, N.E. Suite 300, Atlanta, GA 30326;
www.ritzcarlton.com

Founded: The first Ritz-Carlton hotel opened in Boston in 1927; significant expansion began in 1983

Core business: Guest services

Scope: 34 hotels; 14,000 employees

Key quality practices:

- Quality is seen as a competitive advantage.
- Practices (such as giving employees the authority and tools to correct problems) and personnel (hiring for cultural "fit") are aligned to support service goals.
- Customers define quality.
- Formal quality network to elicit and follow through on ideas.

AVSC International

79 Madison Avenue, New York, NY 10016; www.avsc.org

Founded: 1943

Core business: Making quality reproductive health care services safe and available

Scope: 266 employees; 29 countries; $39 million (1997)

Key quality practices:

- Look at practices from the client's perspective.
- Act as a facilitator, not an enforcer.
- Mix quantitative data collection with qualitative interviews.

- Regular use of structured self-assessment and improvement tools.

"The COPE process is owned by the people who do it. . . . It uses the wisdom of the experts, who are the people who work in that clinic and the people who use those services."

Wellspring House

Wellspring House, 302 Essex Ave., Gloucester, MA 01930

Founded: 1980 as a community organization dedicated to living its ideals

Core business: Engaging deeply with the social and economic causes of disenfranchisement

Scope: 26 dwellings; 24 employees; $1 million annual expenditures (1997)

Key quality practices:

- Focus not only on internal practices, but surrounding environment.
- Engage "clients," stakeholders, and the community in assessment and implementation processes.
- Use the "associative" nature of the organization as a resource to remain close to the clients and the community.
- Emphasis on improvement, not on shortcomings.

"It's part of our culture to constantly reflect on what we are doing and to analyze the causes of the situations."

ADDITIONAL READING

Hackman, J. Richard and Ruth Wagerman. "TQM: Empirical, Conceptual, and Practical Issues," *Administration Science Quarterly*, Vol. 40, Spring 1995, pp. 309–342.

Heskett, James L. "Lessons in the Service Sector," *Harvard Business Review*, March–April 1987, pp. 118–126.

Heskett, James L., W. Earl Sasser, Jr., and Christopher W.L. Hart. *Service Breakthroughs: Changing the Rules of the Game.* New York: Free Press, 1990.

Kennedy, Larry W. *Quality Management in the Nonprofit World: Combining Compassion and Performance to Meet Client Needs and Improve Finances.* San Francisco: Jossey-Bass Publishers, 1991.

Martin, Lawrence L. and Peter M. Kettner. *Measuring the Performance of Human Service Programs.* Thousand Oaks, CA: Sage Publications, 1996.

Shetty, Y.K. and Vernon M. Buehler, eds. *Quality, Productivity, and Innovation: Strategies for Gaining Competitive Advantage.* New York: Elsevier, 1987.

Zacharakis-Jutz, Jeff and Stanley Gajenayake. "Participatory Evaluation's Potential Among Nonprofit Organizations," *Adult Learning,* July/August 1994, pp. 11–14.

ENDNOTES

[1]Originally Access to Voluntary and Safe Contraception, the organization now goes only by AVSC to accommodate its broader mission of promoting public and reproductive health. AVSC International is the largest U.S.-based organization working to improve access to quality family planning and reproductive health services worldwide.

[2]*COPE: Client-Oriented Provider Efficient Services* (New York: AVSC International, 1995).

[3]Paolo Freire, *A Pedagogy of the Oppressed* (New York: Continuum Publishing, 1996).

CHAPTER FOUR

Product Development: Better Ideas and Better Implementation

FRAMING QUESTIONS

▶ How could the nonprofit sector generate better ideas and better programs?

▶ How can the sector develop innovativeness in organizations, as well as entrepreneurs?

▶ How can product development not only support new ideas, but help refine existing ones?

Although society has come to count on the ability of the nonprofit sector to develop programs that respond effectively to public problems, nonprofit program development frequently takes place in a black box. We rely on the programs that come out of the box, but pay little attention to the program-development processes at work inside it. This chapter explores the possibility of an alternative to the black-box approach, asking what nonprofits could achieve by analyzing, investing in, and managing the process of program development more deliberately. The experience of innovative businesses and pathbreaking nonprofits alike suggests that the benefits of more deliberate product development[1] could be significant: not only to create a larger supply of better programs, but also to achieve more success in implementing those programs.

What kind of product-development process yields these results? Excellent product development processes involve more than getting a good idea from the drawing board to the marketplace. The process starts long before the organization has an idea on the drawing board, by helping the organization address the challenge of where and how to find good product ideas in the first place. And excellent product development is not the province of a few product-development specialists. The most successful models engage people throughout the organization in the search for good ideas and the work of turning them into winning products. Finally, the process is used not just to create breakthrough products but also to make continuous improvements that make products more relevant and appealing.

For all its comprehensiveness, a good product development process does not supplant the personal creativity of individuals. To the contrary, the process creates an environment that supports creative, passionate individuals. It imposes discipline and coordination only after the initial inspiration, as the focus shifts to capturing the full potential of an idea by refining it into a winning product. Especially in the nonprofit sector, where we look to social entrepreneurs (often working on their own) for so many program ideas, there might be a tendency to see a formal program development process as an attempt to "bureaucratize" a necessarily chaotic process. But organizations often outgrow the direct reach of their founding entrepreneur. As new and larger groups of people begin developing programs, the organization must face new questions: How are they handling their social challenge? And can they get better at it?

With so many nonprofits invested in generating new ideas, why isn't program development an important organizational process in the nonprofit sector? The problem may lie in a failure to distinguish between *innovations* and *innovativeness*. As Paul Light points out in elaborating on this distinction, the nonprofit sector focuses quite appropriately on innovations by studying the design, impact, and potential for replicating new programs.[2] Unfortunately, innovativeness—how an organization produced an effective program in the first place—gets too little attention. "Most organizations can produce a successful new product occasionally. . . . The question is whether they can sustain or repeat what they did."[3]

Our inquiry suggests both good and bad news about the prospects for improving nonprofits' capacity for innovativeness. The good news is that some thoughtful nonprofit managers are building effective program development processes, precisely because they see how it can help them create good programs and good performance. In some cases, they use the very same strategies as world-class businesses praised for their innovativeness. On the downside, despite its potential for improving nonprofit performance, the process of program development attracts very little funding in an environment that values exemplary programs more than exemplary organizations.

Nonprofit program development approaches, moreover, tend to differ from the for-profit model in one critical way. While businesses stress the benefits of linking idea generation and implementation, nonprofits take the opposite tack: Through program replication and the use of national intermediary organizations, they tend to generate ideas in one set of organizations and implement them in another. This decoupling, which offers important efficiencies, may harm the quality both of programs and of nonprofit organizations. Moving toward a more integrated program development approach therefore implies new organizational practices for both nonprofit managers and funders.

Finally, nonprofits lack a "theory of practice" that could help them build on the assets they do bring to the challenge of program development. There is little discussion among practitioners about how to manage or improve program development. As a result, it is difficult to promote the widespread use of effective organizational processes among nonprofits, or to help those in the vanguard of effective practice support those with shallower capacity.

For three perspectives on product development, we turn to a composite business model that describes the processes used by leading companies, and two nonprofit examples of deliberate, formal program development processes: the Boston YWCA and the Vera Institute of Justice.

A WORLD-CLASS BUSINESS MODEL FOR PRODUCT DEVELOPMENT

P. Ranganath Nayak,[4] a vice president at Boston Consulting Group and a student of innovation and product development, describes the four characteristics of product development processes used by world-class companies:

1. They treat product development as an *organizational process* that can be structured, measured, and improved.
2. They harness talent and perspectives in the company through the use of *cross-functional teams*.
3. They put *customers at the center* of the product development process, both by encouraging direct contact between company employees and customers, and through new methods of in-depth market research.
4. They support the *passion and creativity* of employees by creating conducive work environments.

Together, these approaches support a more efficient and effective product development process.

Product Development as an Organizational Process

"Managing inspiration" with a disciplined, measurable process might seem like an oxymoron. Many businesses have learned, however, that the costs of product development can be measured, and, once measured, reduced.

> *"Managing inspiration" with a disciplined, measurable process might seem like an oxymoron, but it works.*

In the automotive industry, for example, Ford Motor Company wanted to reduce its new car development timeline from six years to the three-and-a-half years of its Japanese competitors. General

Motors wanted to reduce investments in new car development from $4 billion per model to Honda's $2 billion. To improve the efficiency of their product development, companies begin by defining a series of product development milestones. At these key moments, managers review progress on the development of a product and determine whether to continue: Is a concept refined enough to go on to prototype development, or has a prototype been tested well enough to move to scale production? These milestones provide the foundation of a highly structured process. Over time, the organization can use these approaches not only to develop better products but to measure and improve the performance of the product development process itself for long-term success.

Integrated, Cross-Functional Team

According to Nayak, the single biggest efficiency improvement in product development comes from the introduction of integrated, cross-functional product development teams. The traditional product development approach resembles an assembly line. For example, one group might propose a product concept, which is then passed on to the marketing staff for judgments about sales potential, after which it might go to engineering for prototype development, and then on to manufacturing for consideration of mass-production options. Higher level managers then review this cumulative body of incremental choices and make a single "go" or "no go" decision on whether to move the prototype to full-scale development.

The development of "autonomous teams with a great deal of empowerment," Nayak argues, produces dramatically better results. An integrated team, including, for example, engineering, marketing, and manufacturing, eliminates the long chain of pass-offs by assessing and refining ideas together. Instead of finding out late in the process (i.e., after time and effort are expended by design, marketing, and sales) that a product idea poses nearly insurmountable manufacturing problems, an integrated team learns about the problem *during* the design process, when it can respond immediately. Instead of turning back to start over, or worse, proceeding with flawed plans, the team can develop modifications before investing more time and effort in the project.

Connecting Companies and Customers in New Ways

After instituting many of these process improvements, Nayak's world-class companies then turned their attention to the "fuzzy front end" of product development. Here, says Nayak, "you're not sure exactly where all the ideas are coming from, how to screen them, how to boil them down to a finite number, and get to the point where you know what you want to create." The front-end challenge is not to turn ideas into products, but to generate better ideas in the first place. Managers often neglect this part of the process for two reasons: It is hardly visible, and it seems to have few costs associated with it. Instead, managers tend to pay attention later in the process, when each additional step imposes more costs and where the penalties for modifying ideas increases sharply. But with the right front-end process, companies can generate better ideas initially, submitting only the best to the more expensive tail-end development process. (See Exhibit 4-1.)

Customers hold the key to a successful front-end process. Traditionally, the pool of new product ideas is fed by a company's idea generators (e.g., engineers, chemists, or technical talent) and its marketing department. After the technicians generate tentative product concepts, the marketing staff uses surveys, focus groups, one-on-one interviews, and consumer trend analysis to judge how consumers will respond. Alternatively, market research can provide technicians with insight into trends and consumer preferences that might inspire new product ideas.

The new approach always starts with customers. First, and most directly, employees at world-class companies talk to customers directly. Nayak is convinced that you get the really brilliant ideas when people who don't normally meet with customers—"the nerds who sit in the laboratories and do engineering"—go out into the marketplace and meet with customers and have in-depth conversations with them. Market research becomes everyone's business.

Second, excellent companies focus less on customers' reactions to existing ideas and more on discerning latent needs. These are the unarticulated desires for things not yet created. Nayak's study of breakthrough products shows, for example, that no consumer ever reported wanting "a high fidelity portable radio/cassette player" until the appearance of the Sony Walkman. Getting at these latent

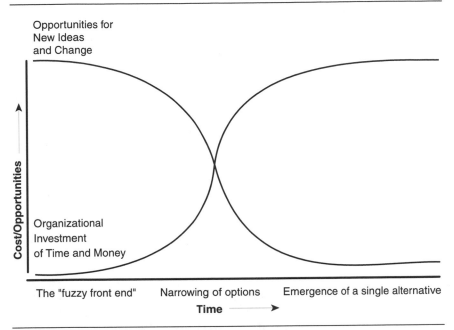

Exhibit 4–1 In traditional product development, an increasing amount of attention and resources are invested in one idea as time passes. This often locks the organization into a limited set of choices, and prevents alternatives from emerging.

needs, however, requires new market research methods that probe customers' needs and lifestyles more deeply. A company working on household products, for example, might assign researchers to follow a domestic cleaner all day, observing in sustained detail how he works and what his latent needs might be.

Third, companies are engaging "lead adopters" directly in their product development work. For example, a Swiss manufacturer of the hardware used in hanging pipes and utility conduits wanted to boost sales by improving its product. The breakthrough came when the company discovered that some pipe hangers were already improving their product by making minor retrofits during installation. The company hired a group of these pipe hangers for two days to help develop improvements that later proved critical to improving sales.

Supporting Passion

A customer-focused front end and a disciplined and structured tail end cannot substitute for creativity itself. And although organizations cannot manufacture the raw material of creativity, the outstanding ones have devised ways to create an environment that stimulates, supports, and rewards creativity and passion. Nayak cites Microsoft and Bell Labs (now part of Lucent Technologies), as examples.

> *The raw material of creativity can't be manufactured, but excellent organizations have figured out how to nurture its growth and development.*

Microsoft organizes its workplace like a campus. The environment and culture support employees' desire to pursue work with what Nayak calls "a kind of spiritual intensity." Stock options do motivate employees, says Nayak, but their passion for creating new ideas is even more powerful. With untraditional hours, workplace sleeping quarters, and on-site laundry services, Microsoft offers the amenities needed to allow creative people to focus on their passion. Bell Labs attempts to nourish opportunities for creative insight by keeping different types of researchers and specialists working near each other, with maximum chance for informal interaction about their respective work.

From these practices emerges a picture of product development not as an assembly line, but as a funnel. At the open front end, a number of good ideas swirl around within an organization, in an environment that encourages passion and collaboration. A single idea does not emerge as a winner right from the start. Instead, the ideas spiral down the funnel, where the formal, designated check-ins provide the discipline for winnowing and refining. As ideas progress toward the narrow implementation end, their merits and prospects are continually reviewed and improved until the product is brought to market. The process does not end there; other ideas are already working their way through the funnel, and existing

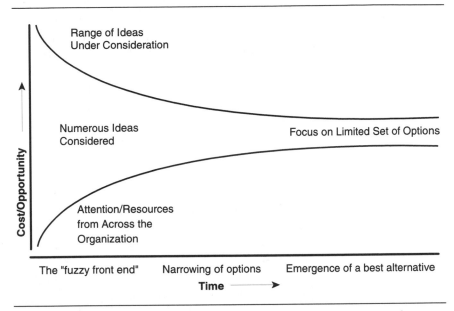

Exhibit 4–2   Using a "funnel" process for product development, more ideas are considered at the beginning of the process. Good management of the "fuzzy front end" allows for consideration and refinement of a variety of options before too many resources are dedicated to any one idea.

products will go through the process periodically as part of a continuous improvement program. (See Exhibit 4-2.)

THE BOSTON YWCA'S YOUTH VOICE COLLABORATIVE

Ruth Irving-Parham, deputy director for operations of the Boston YWCA, views the process used to develop the Youth Voice Collaborative (YVC), a program that combines media education and mentoring to increase the leadership skills and self-esteem of teenagers, as "a model that we can use to develop all new programs." Participants in YVC work with each other and adult mentors to review and critique news reporting, produce their own stories for print and broadcast, and learn about communications technology.

The program began through contact with individual customers and institutional collaborators. YWCA president Marti Wilson-

Taylor, after reading a 1994 Carnegie Task Force report documenting the number of out-of-school hours many children and teens spend unsupervised, contacted three other youth-serving agencies that were also exploring ways to engage youth. While considering ways for them to collaborate, Wilson-Taylor attended a panel on youth issues. There, she heard a young woman explain why she wasn't in a gang: "I was, but I walked into the Boys and Girls Club, picked up a camcorder, and it changed my life." At that point, says Irving-Parham, "it all made sense: Media would engage youngsters like very few other things could."

Both to develop the idea and to get buy-in from the individuals and organizations needed to implement it, the YWCA and its partner organizations convened a planning group. This group eventually numbered about 40, including representatives of youth-serving agencies, the Boston public schools, local universities, media professionals (both technical experts and journalists), and young people. With the help of a $40,000 foundation planning grant, the committee engaged a process consultant to help them develop a set of principles to manage the challenge of product-development-by-committee. Most significantly, in Irving-Parham's view, the group agreed to two principles: pledging to be learners throughout, which for many meant learning about the Internet and other communications technologies; and involving young people every step of the way. The group also agreed to explore program replication options, in the hope of generating fees to support the program.

Several subcommittees organized research efforts to inform the program planning. Students from Harvard's Graduate School of Education were commissioned to conduct a literature search on similar programs. Another group assessed funding feasibility. Another drafted curriculum plans. And a group of college students conducted focus groups with teenagers. By the end, YVC had emerged as a clearly defined program model that enjoyed enthusiastic support from a number of key organizations and potential mentors.

After a six-month pilot test of the program, during which a group of teenagers successfully researched and produced a radio program on poverty, the group launched a one-year demonstration effort.

Already, a documentary produced by an 18-year-old YVC partici-
pant, "Too Many Joses," has aired on public television. The YWCA
had considered the possibility of replication almost from the outset,
and will pursue that course if the demonstration proves successful.

VERA INSTITUTE OF JUSTICE

The Vera Institute of Justice, a 36-year-old nonprofit, designs and
operates demonstration programs (typically for government agencies) as a means of improving justice in the United States. Christopher Stone, president of Vera, cites the development of the
Immigration Appearance Assistance Project as an example of their
program development process.

The U.S. Immigration and Naturalization Service (INS) approached Vera for help resolving a capacity problem: on any given
day, it had 80,000 people in deportation proceedings, but only 8,000
beds in its detention facilities. Of the 72,000 who were not detained,
many would eventually receive orders for deportation. By then,
they would be unlikely to turn themselves in, and it would be too
expensive to track them down.

In response to this problem, INS initially wanted Vera to design
a program of community supervision for those people it had
decided to release. But Vera analysts judged that approach, on its
own, to be unrealistic. Some of those who violated the supervision
needed to be detained, not released, and this would decrease the
system's efficiency. Vera made a counterproposal: It would create a
community supervision program along with a new screening system for detention, allowing the INS to use its detention space more
efficiently while improving compliance by those it released. This
approach would not only improve INS efficiency, it would also
serve Vera's mission of improving justice.

Planning for the INS program took five months and was funded
with a $125,000 grant. Four staff, two already at Vera and two
recruited for their special knowledge of the project area, devoted
their efforts full-time to the project. Vera begins all projects with a
planning process in which it learns about the client agency, defines

the problems and opportunities, and establishes a program concept. The Vera program staff proposed rationalizing the use of the detention space through a screening process. An immigrant entering the system would be assessed to determine whether it was reasonably safe to release him, and whether he had an incentive (such as hope of winning his case) to appear for hearings. Detention space would be reserved for those most at risk of escape or harm. With fewer low-risk people detained for long periods, Vera hoped the new system would be both more efficient and more just.

After estimating the costs and benefits of the new approach, the Vera staff designed a full demonstration, with designated milestones where outcomes and performance would be assessed and the program could be improved. The completed program plan was sent for review and discussion to an institute meeting, where all Vera's other project directors, all of its planners and researchers, and key administrative officers examined it. The plan went next to Vera's board, which focused on several key questions: Does the program serve Vera's mission by improving justice? Have staff identified all the risks? Will Vera have the capacity to manage them?

Despite some skepticism among INS district directors and civil servants, the agency accepted a design for a three-year demonstration, to be funded at $2 million per year. Two of the four staff who developed the plan were deployed to operate it, with Vera handling oversight and the back office administrative functions.

As with all Vera projects, the staff recruited a national advisory board of academics, experts, and practitioners from several locations outside New York. Vera hopes that, in addition to offering constructive advice during two annual meetings, advisory board members will become proponents for promising projects. A team of researchers led by a Columbia University economist is developing and conducting an intensive evaluation of the project. After internal review by Vera staff at predesignated milestones, the project will be submitted annually for board review.

If the Appearance Project outcomes are promising, the project staff will develop an institutionalization plan, proposing methods for implementing the reform and designing a technical assistance component that Vera would offer to help early adopters operate the program. While the project moves through the pipeline, Vera will be using a similar process to develop or demonstrate eight additional programs.

USING WORLD-CLASS PRODUCT DEVELOPMENT FOR NONPROFIT ENDS

These examples reveal striking parallels between the nonprofit and world-class business approaches to program and product development. Clearly, the YWCA and Vera value formal program development processes as an important part of advancing their social missions. The particulars of their approaches, moreover, suggest that they have discovered and applied some of the very same practices touted in the business world. For example, both organizations use cross-functional teams to solicit ideas and gain a broader perspective about the value and design of programs. The YWCA's planning committee is a textbook example. Vera's "institute meetings," though less central to the generation of ideas, provide the benefits of team thinking at critical moments in the review of a proposed program.

The nonprofits have also integrated extensive client contact into their idea generation. The YWCA's original inspiration came from an encounter, in the field, between the CEO and a young person. The process that followed deliberately included young people as lead adopters who could provide ideas and feedback as the program was designed. Vera also makes use of extensive client contact. Vera includes public managers in its advisory committees to engage them on the ground floor of product development. On another project, investigating the causes and dynamics of youth violence, Vera has assigned ethnographers to undertake continuous, long-term, on-the-ground study of young people's daily lives. This search for latent knowledge is likely to be decisive in shaping subsequent program development.

In some respects, nonprofits have assets especially well-suited to excellent program development. Nonprofits are probably better positioned than most businesses to pursue both teamwork and client focus, since those values correspond to the goals of collaboration and service to which many nonprofits aspire. Also, the supply of passion in nonprofits provides enormous advantage for program development: Many people are attracted to nonprofits precisely because of deeply held convictions and commitments.

REFRAMING PROGRAM DEVELOPMENT AS AN ORGANIZATIONAL PROCESS

Put Program Development Processes on the Nonprofit Agenda

The sector has invested heavily in refining the processes of replication and evaluation. It could supplement what it has learned by paying similar attention to the earlier phases of program development. Toward that end, many of the intermediaries that now work on program development could compare how they handle program development across specialties. Researchers could analyze the processes used to develop programs that prove highly effective to see how the fuzzy front-end process might have contributed to better outcomes. They could also try to determine how strong program development processes strengthen or improve a nonprofit in other ways.

Invest in the "Fuzzy Front End" of Program Development

In for-profits and nonprofits alike, the fuzzy front end of product development poses the same dilemma. Management's attention to and funding for product development tends to come too late, after lots of time and money have already been spent, making it more difficult to change the new product substantially. Businesses have solved this problem by increasing customer contact and creating cross-functional teams to help them discover and test the best ideas early on.

Nonprofits can, and often do, use similar approaches: Intensive client contact, in the form of focus groups, work with lead adopters, and constant interaction with clients is both possible and desirable. But this is exactly the type of work that goes under- or unfunded. Grants tend to come when the program idea is already well developed and it's time for pilot programs, demonstrations, and evaluations. Funders and nonprofits need to consider earlier interventions.

One solution may be for nonprofits to identify a target population or issue and seek market research grants to fund in-depth exploration. Some foundations now offer nonprofits planning grants to investigate potential programs, but these are often awarded to test a specific program through interviews and research. At the true fuzzy front end, nonprofits could investigate latent client needs that might lead to better focused concepts. Funding for this early phase could stress the need for thoughtful research, and put less emphasis on fast turnaround of new ideas.

For example, the Vera Institute is now conducting in-depth field research on the causes and dynamics of violence among youth. Instead of testing a specific program, they will track over several years the lives of a select number of inner-city teenagers. This research likely will give Vera's program designers powerful insight into the types of programs that might be useful. On a smaller scale and budget, other nonprofits could define similar research to inform both their own program development and grantmaking at a foundation.

Build Program Development Processes—Not Just Programs

Although our analysis suggests problems in the tendency to centralize the best program development capacity in a very few places, we are not arguing that the nonprofit sector should ignore the efficiencies of scale that intermediaries can generate. Foundations, intermediaries, national membership organizations, and federations all play critical roles in developing important new programs. But they can have an even greater impact by also helping nonprofits develop their own program development capacity.

Could Vera and the YWCA, for example, help the implementers of their innovations by helping them develop their own capacity for innovativeness? Obviously, not every program originator could or should become a generic program development consultant, but the most innovative and sophisticated program developers clearly have much to teach. They could explain their own methods, play a coaching and consulting role to nonprofits developing their own programs, and help the organizations prepare not just to implement new programs but to improve them intelligently through a process of continuous improvement.

> *Nonprofits are probably better positioned than most businesses to pursue both teamwork and customer focus.*

For all the similarities between the best business and nonprofit approaches, critical differences can affect the potential of these approaches in improving social outcomes. First, highly developed management processes like these are exceptional in the nonprofit sector. The YWCA's effort was the first of its kind in the organization's 138-year history, and Vera's sophisticated capacity has been developed precisely because most government agencies and nonprofits lack its program design expertise.

The nonprofit sector, moreover, has no "theory of practice" to help organizations develop and improve their approaches. In effect, Nayak's model emerges from a decades-long search, including research, field work, teaching, and consulting, that has given business managers ever more useful concepts with which to design and improve their own processes. In contrast, virtually every nonprofit seeking better program development processes must become a trailblazer. There are simply no well developed nonprofit concepts for managing and designing effective program development processes, just an unconnected assortment of program development practices with little attention to the value and possibility of articulating and promoting coherent processes that can be analyzed and improved. Even the best formal program development processes in the sector may go unappreciated, because few nonprofit leaders have the opportunity to discuss them. Without knowledge-sharing mechanisms and a theory of practice, it is difficult to build on the sector's assets and potential for more effective program development.

> *Virtually every nonprofit seeking better program development processes must become a trailblazer.*

But the question remains: If these processes are relevant for non-profits, why isn't the nonprofit sector investing more in them?

Investing in Program Development Capacity

Most nonprofits simply do not have the funds and staff to pursue program development in a formal, sophisticated way. In the competition for funds, low overhead and administrative costs are a competitive advantage. So a nonprofit, in effect, needs to limit its capacity for organizational processes like program development in order to compete effectively. On the for-profit side, many businesses face similar pressures but are beginning to reject aggressive cost-cutting strategies in favor of investment in capacity-building.

> *By cutting too much, businesses developed "organizational anorexia," a condition more often the norm than a disorder for nonprofits.*

Nonprofits, moreover, don't always grow by developing new programs or improving existing ones, and are therefore unlikely to assess their need for program development capacity. Whereas many for-profit managers rely on new or improved products to achieve greater market share, nonprofit managers can grow their organizations by exploiting the capacity to deliver *existing* programs. They bid for more contracts or grants to provide a given service or program. Particularly in the case of government contracts, nonprofits are funded to deliver, not develop programs. Their capacity for program development and enhancement is not a competitive advantage.

It may be easier, moreover, to develop a new nonprofit organization than to develop a new program within existing nonprofits. Many innovative new programs enter the nonprofit sector in the form of new organizations; a breakthrough program typically grows a nonprofit around it. It may be far less often that a non-profit organization creates a breakthrough program. The for-profit sector also has an impressive record of entrepreneurial successes, where product breakthroughs also lead to the creation of new companies, but businesses are more attentive to the possibilities for creating new products *within* an organization. At a time when many worry that we may have too many small nonprofits competing for funds, establishing separate infrastructures and fragmenting the approach to social problems, it may be wise to consider whether we give employees with new ideas the latitude or support to launch them within existing nonprofits. But as long as building organizational capacity for work like this in existing nonprofits is perceived as padding the budget, funders are more likely to support the startups.

> *Breakthrough programs create nonprofit organizations; few nonprofits create breakthrough programs.*

Finally, the nonprofit sector has what seems like a viable alternative to investing in widespread program development capacity: program replication. In part because of the high value the sector places on cooperation, the discovery of one nonprofit organization can be readily shared with others. And as long as breakthroughs can be shared (with the help of foundations and nonprofit associations), building widespread program development capacity might appear unnecessary. But the for-profit model suggests that decoupling the capacity for innovation and the capacity for implementation can limit the prospects for impact.

Decoupling Idea-Generation and Implementation: Penny-Wise, Pound Foolish?

Current for-profit approaches to product development emphasize the advantages of linking idea generation and implementation. They believe front-line staff and technical people should work hand-in-hand for several reasons. First, front-line workers are an invaluable source of ideas about customer needs and preferences, as well as about product performance or service quality. Second, the cross-functional teams are effective only when they draw on idea people and implementers alike to develop better products. Concepts can be improved as marketers, manufacturers, customer service representatives, and engineers all work together to convert an idea into a viable product. Third, the practices of good product development—which involves customer focus and responsiveness, an emphasis on learning, support for passion, and collaboration across the organization—improve the overall performance of the organization. The day of the isolated product development department is over.

The nonprofit sector has frequently taken the opposite approach: It is decoupling idea generation and implementation. This decoupling is evident not only in replication, but also in other forms of centralized program development.

The development of public policy often begins the process of decoupling idea generators and implementers. In many cases, universities or think tanks, based on research they conduct, will recommend new approaches to solving public problems. If elected officials and policy makers accept their recommendations, they then authorize public funding to support implementation of the new approach. Finally, when government agencies contract with nonprofit providers to deliver the service, they often impose the program design that emerged in the upstream research and policy-making process. The idea generators and implementers end up separated by several layers of public policy making.

Many funders and practitioners, moreover, have concluded that not every nonprofit needs formal program development capacity. To conserve scarce resources, these capacities have been developed in a few strategically located intermediary organizations that share their findings widely. The Vera Institute is a good example of centralized program development capacity. Over its 36-year history, it has developed a formal, sophisticated, relatively well-funded program development process. Its new program for the Immigration and Naturalization Service, for example, was developed by Vera in New York City, but could have a national impact if it is implemented at all INS regional agencies.

> *The nonprofit sector is decoupling idea generation and implementation.*

The same logic explains the mission of other intermediaries that develop and test new programs on behalf of a wider field of nonprofits or government agencies. National organizations such as the Child Welfare League provide these services for their members. These intermediaries can either publicize the programs, allowing others to learn from them or provide hands-on technical assistance to other nonprofit organizations operating them. In addition, foundations often act as idea generators, designing programs and issuing RFPs to attract nonprofit implementers.

This decoupling of idea generation and implementation poses special problems in the program development process. First, central program developers are poorly situated to use customers as a source of ideas. Field trips, focus groups, and client advisory committees might compensate for some of the limitations, but they are hardly the same as directly involving front-line workers, and clients themselves, in the process. Second, central program development cannot take advantage of cross-functional teams. The people who will deliver the service, raise funds to support it, and train new staff to deliver it all work downstream in the implementing nonprofit, while idea people work on their own.

Additionally, as Gregg Petersmeyer, a student of innovation and community-based social entrepreneurs, points out, the central organizations of the nonprofit sector have mastered formal, technical processes, but usually are too far from the front-line action to bring passion to bear on their work. "These are not the same people who actually invest their energy during 16-hour days to implement programs," says Petersmeyer.

The biggest consequence of this decoupling may lie not in the central program development organizations, but in the implementing nonprofits. With little or no program development capacity, effective *implementation* may become more elusive. Consider the YWCA case: Their program development capacity generated a good program *and* supported good implementation. Like many innovations, the Youth Voice Collaborative is not a radical breakthrough, but a creative recombination of existing ideas. It includes mentoring, youth journalism as a form of empowerment, and technology and media literacy. It engages young people in constructive activity that develops their potential.

Most innovations are not radical breakthroughs, but creative recombinations of existing ideas.

What stands out about the program is the performance of the YWCA, both in creating and implementing the program. It marshaled the resources and leadership to engage in an ambitious process of thinking, researching, and experimenting that led to the program. It tapped into the passions of its staff and committee members; placed a premium on engaging and responding to youth; and attracted funders, supporters, collaborators, and visibility as a result of its quality efforts. It's not surprising, given the quality of these inputs, that the program outputs were so well received. Yet the YWCA's inclination was to replicate the program through a licensing arrangement or technical assistance program, either of which would have had the salutary effect of generating revenues to support the original program. But spreading the YWCA's ambitious program development process, not the program alone, might produce a greater impact among the organizations implementing new programs.

The solution is not to stop investing in central program development, or in replication, but to create complementary capacities in central organizations and implementing organizations. Specialized knowledge powerhouses are essential to continue to generate research and knowledge, but some program development capacity is essential for operating nonprofits as well. In order to serve their communities over the long term, they need innovativeness, not just innovations.

Effective program development processes, moreover, support not only breakthrough innovations, but also incremental improvements to existing programs. Nonprofits often discuss the need for "local adaptation" of program models so they will better meet the particular needs of a local community. But the discussion rarely includes an analysis of what capacities would help local operators *effectively* adapt a program without compromising its efficacy. The key features of good product development processes, especially the focus on customers and support for creative workers who can collaborate in teams, position an organization to make effective improvements. As an organization assesses the changing needs of its constituents, and considers how new research might affect its program design, it can make modifications to those programs over time.

CONCLUSION

In the final analysis, strengthening the nonprofit sector's capacity for either breakthrough programs or continuous program improvements will require more attention to program development as a deliberate organizational process. The alternative—a *de facto* approach where inspiration and intuition produce consistently good outcomes—is effective only for those who have it. Something that cannot be analyzed and captured as a set of principles and practices cannot help nonprofits that do want to improve their performance. Developing their capacity requires assessing, adapting, and building on the underlying principles that have consistently produced good results for highly effective organizations.

ORGANIZATION PROFILES

"World-class" businesses
(based on P. Ranganath Nayak's model)
- Make product development an organizational process.
- Create integrated, cross-functional teams.
- Connect companies and customers.

- Support passion and creativity.

"Autonomous teams with a great deal of empowerment."

YWCA of Greater Boston/Youth Voice Collaborative

140 Clarendon Street, Boston, MA 02116; www.yvc.org

Founded: YWCA Boston founded in 1866; Youth Voice Collaborative project begun in 1994

Core business: Creating opportunities for women's leadership (YWCA); helping young people develop media literacy to amplify their voices and contribute to their community (YVC).

Scope: YWCA has 80 employees, serves 10,000 mostly women and girls a year; $4.7 million budget (1997). YVC has 4 employees; serves 100 youth per year; $200,000 budget (1997).

Key program development practices:

- Identify "latent" client needs.
- Build support among and encourage involvement of key stake-holders.
- Involve constituents.
- Engage all participants in a learning process.

"Involving young people every step of the way."

Vera Institute of Justice

377 Broadway, New York, NY 10013; www.vera.org

Founded: 1961, as the Manhattan Bail Project

Core business: Designing and implementing innovative programs that encourage just practices

Scope: 135 employees; 4 projects currently underway; $9.2 million budget (1996–97)

Key program development practices:

- Respond to the deeper need, not the immediate request.
- Designate milestones in the development process.
- Build dissemination opportunities into the process.
- Involve "outside" reviewers.

"From the moment a new idea has promise, the design of a demonstration is a close collaboration between practitioners and researchers. . . ."

ADDITIONAL READING

Bacon, Jr., Frank R. and Thomas W. Butler, Jr. *Planned Innovation: A Dynamic Approach to Strategic Planning and the Successful Development of New Products*. Ann Arbor, MI: University of Michigan, Institute of Science and Technology, 1981.

Daugherty, Deborah, and Cynthia Hardy. "Sustained Product Innovation in Large, Mature Organizations: Overcoming Innovation-to-Organization Problems," *Academy of Management Journal*, 1996, Vol. 39, No. 5, pp. 1120–1153.

Deschamps, Jean-Philippe, and P. Ranganath Nayak. *Product Juggernauts: How Companies Mobilize to Generate a Stream of Market Winners*. Boston: Harvard Business School Press, 1995.

Light, Paul C. *Sustaining Innovation: Creating Nonprofit and Government Organizations That Innovate Naturally*. San Francisco: Jossey-Bass, 1998.

Lorsch, Jay. *Product Innovation and Organization*. New York: Macmillan, 1965.

Zegans, Marc. *Innovation, Strategy and Inertia: Unbundling Some Old Assumptions*. Cambridge, MA: Taubman Center, JFK School of Government, Harvard University, 1990.

ENDNOTES

[1]Product development refers to goods or services; the same process supports both. In this chapter, we treat for-profit product development and nonprofit program development as parallel processes.

[2]Paul C. Light, *Sustaining Innovation: Creating Nonprofit and Government Organizations That Innovate Naturally*.(San Francisco: Jossey-Bass, 1998).

[3]Deborah Daugherty and Cynthia Hardy, "Sustained Product Innovation in Large, Mature Organizations: Overcoming Innovation-to-Organization Problems," *Academy of Management Journal*, Vol. 39, No. 5, 1996, pp. 1120–1153.

[4]See Jean-Philippe Deschamps and P. Ranganath Nayak, *Product Juggernauts: How Companies Mobilize to Generate a Stream of Market Winners* (Boston: Harvard Business School Press, 1995).

CHAPTER FIVE

Benchmarking: An Organizational Process That Links Learning and Results

FRAMING QUESTIONS

- ▶ How can we know if we're doing a good job?
- ▶ For whom is our work important?
- ▶ What are the traits of successful performance?
- ▶ How could we think about getting better?

The nonprofit sector understands well the value of learning for creating effective programs, and has invested considerable effort in several learning approaches. For example, many nonprofits and their funders support training and professional development, which improves critically important individual skill sets. Recently, nonprofits have focused on identifying and disseminating "best practices," usually in the form of effective programs and strategies that organizations share with each other to advance their work. Conferences, publications, and even awards all highlight and publicize best practices. This best-practice approach, however, consigns learners to a passive role—hearing about what others have defined as success—and, more significant, tends to leave off where the hard work of implementing good ideas begins. To get from "best practices" to "better performance" requires an *organizational* learning tool.

> *Benchmarking helps bridge the gap between great ideas and great performance.*

Benchmarking is an organizational learning process that bridges the gap between great ideas and great performance. In benchmarking, an organization that has defined an opportunity for improved performance identifies another organization (or unit within its own organization) that has achieved better results and conducts a systematic study of the other organization's achievements, practices, and processes. The benchmarking process then goes further to include the development and implementation of strategies that will help the organization improve its performance. Because of its focus on exemplary performance, benchmarking is sometimes referred to as "best practices." But benchmarking is more than just discovering best practices; it includes comparative measurement, active goal-setting, and implementation. Benchmarking finds appropriate best practices and puts them into action.

Businesses began exploiting benchmarking when they realized that they might not be asking the right questions. In the traditional competitive analysis that preceded benchmarking, companies looked at competitors' products to see how their product design might be superior. Many came to see that competitive advantage is created by a combination of factors, including the time it takes to get a product from design to market, the total cost of the process, the nature of the process, systems for managing and motivating employees, and customers' judgments about value. Benchmarking helps organizations learn exactly where their performance lags and focuses them on the application of best practices.

The benchmarking cases recounted here show not only the power of this tool in improving performance, but also the issues that surface for nonprofits in using it effectively. The shift to active, organizational learning requires attention to measurement, analysis of deficiencies, comparisons with better performing organizations, and an investment of time and resources—all, as nonprofit leaders know well, practices that cut against the grain of many nonprofit cultures and funding environments.

XEROX CORPORATION

The Xerox Corporation, the world's largest manufacturer of copy machines and a leading producer of computers, is recognized as a benchmarking pioneer. Xerox began experimenting with benchmarking in the late 1970s, when its Japanese competitors emerged with lower-cost, high-quality products backed by strong customer service. In this intensely competitive environment, learning was a matter of survival.

Oddly, however, Xerox's critical benchmarking breakthrough came not by focusing on the competitors who threatened it, but by looking to a best-in-its-class company from another industry altogether. Xerox understood that performance issues are often a function of generic organizational processes, not just product design. Xerox had targeted slow order-fulfillment, a complaint of many customers and a top priority for improvement. In focusing on this process, a senior manager suddenly realized, from personal experience, that L.L. Bean, the catalog clothing company, could move from receipt of a customer order on the phone to product delivery in a very short time. To better understand the best practices behind this success, Xerox headed for L.L. Bean's headquarters in Freeport, Maine—not to its competitors in Tokyo. (Presumably, it also helped that L.L. Bean, flattered by the attentions of a giant multinational, was not a competitor.)

Since that time, Xerox has embraced benchmarking as an active learning tool and has urged managers throughout the company to adopt it. Former chairman David T. Kearns promoted benchmarking as a core practice. He defined it as "the continuous process of measuring our products, services, and practices against our toughest competitors or those companies renowned as leaders. " As customer services benchmarking manager Warren Jeffries explains, benchmarking at Xerox is still very much a matter of competitive advantage. It is used to "keep Xerox's edge razor-sharp. . . to discover where something is being done with less time, lower cost, fewer resources, and better technology." (See Exhibit 5-1 for a summary of the benchmarking process used by Xerox.)

Benchmarking begins with learning. Xerox identifies a problem in its organization or discovers something that someone else does better. To do this, of course, Xerox must measure its own performance. Without information about its own practices, processes, and results, it could not identify a gap to close. Therefore, Jeffries counsels organizations interested in benchmarking to "know yourself" as a first step.

Xerox's approach to benchmarking puts processes first and metrics second. For example, Xerox may discover that a competitor produces a copier whose outer shell costs $1,000. The shell for a com-

---

Planning
1. Identify product, service, or process to be benchmarked.
2   Identify comparative organizations.
3. Determine data collection method and collect data.

Analysis
4. Determine current performance "gaps."
5. Project future performance levels.

Integration
6. Communicate benchmark findings and gain acceptance.
7. Establish improvement goals.

Action
8. Develop action plans.
9. Implement specific actions and monitor progress.
10. Recalibrate benchmarks.

Exhibit 5–1   The Xerox benchmarking process.

parable Xerox product is $1,200. Xerox will use the difference in cost not as an automatic goal, but as a signal to look at the production and purchasing processes that result in those shell costs to discover the sources of the difference and to determine if action is needed.

> *In most organizations, there is a tendency for* doing *to eclipse* planning, *and* planning *to eclipse* learning.

Although Xerox is an acknowledged leader in this practice, and has been since 1979, it must remain vigilant about keeping the practice in continual use throughout the organization. In most organizations, there is a tendency for *doing* to eclipse *planning*, and *planning* to eclipse *learning*. In Xerox, these tendencies are countered with visible and frequent reinforcement by top management, investment in a position such as Jeffries', and commitment to training in the use of benchmarking.

CARE USA

Benchmarking doesn't always mean looking for best practices in other organizations. As CARE USA discovered, valuable information is often available through internal comparisons. CARE USA is the largest international nonprofit organization devoted to meeting the needs of the developing world's poor in emergency relief, rehabilitation, and sustainable development. It is also the largest member of an 11-organization world confederation called CARE International. CARE has traditionally operated in water and sanitation, health, population, small business development, and agriculture and natural resources.

CARE is a highly decentralized organization, managing projects through country offices and suboffices in 37 nations. The country offices raise over 80 percent of funding for projects. Most headquarters staff have held positions in the field, and will go back to the field eventually. Total headquarters staff accounts for less than 1 percent of CARE's personnel.

Marc Lindenberg, senior vice president for programs from 1992 to 1997, explains that CARE, which operates in remote and sometimes dangerous areas, has a very strong service culture. People who join CARE are profoundly motivated by the urgency of global problems, and want to deliver services. Their philosophy is often " 'Just do it' rather than 'Let's analyze it.' Nearly half of CARE's work in any given year responds to emergencies like cyclones, famines, and wars. Outsiders sometimes describe our program staff as cowboys and cowgirls," Lindenberg explains. "Their work is dangerous and exhausting, and they believe they have the right to be cynical about detailed analysis and data collection. Many believe that each project is so unique that cross comparisons make no sense."

> *The staff are seen as cowboys and cowgirls who "just do it."*

In 1993, CARE confronted a number of pressures that forced it to challenge this decentralized service culture. Competition for funds in the emergency, relief, and development services world had increased in recent years. A major donor, the U.S. Agency for International Development (US AID), planned to cut back funds over the next few years. CARE was getting feedback from other donors that it was not the only game in town anymore, nor perhaps the best. CARE management responded in part by turning to benchmarking to help it improve the impact of its programs and, in the process, show donors that it could meet the funding "market" challenges.

Consistent with its just-do-it culture, CARE had very little reliable, global data on its overall project portfolios or beneficiary levels to get started on a benchmarking effort. There was virtually no cost-per-participant information on various programs and few baselines for post-project impact assessments. As a first step toward improvement, CARE constructed a pool of information about project performance worldwide.

Initially, CARE took two approaches to benchmarking. In one, headquarters technical staff classified projects by types of interventions, and based on the literature and other organizations' experience, identified best practices. They then ranked the project portfolios to show the percentage of projects at the best-practice level. Using this information, they nudged and sometimes pushed project managers toward improvement. The second approach was more participatory. Headquarters technical groups organized workshops with project managers and jointly identified the keys to best practices. They then had project managers evaluate their own projects and develop self-improvement plans. They also organized "lessons learned" and "lessons applied" seminars.

For example, the analysis of water projects began with the creation of performance indicators that would describe a successful outcome. Since the water projects aim to create a sustainable water supply that supports better health, the indicators focused on longer-term maintenance of the systems, along with local health conditions, captured, for example, by the incidence of diarrhea. (See Exhibit 5-2 for a list of indicators.) Staff gathered information on these indicators, as well as on project costs, for 31 systems with similar characteristics. From this information, those with both high efficiency and high impact emerged as best-practice systems. With a relatively large database and considerable variation in performance, CARE could conduct an internal benchmarking process that allowed it to learn from, and benefit, its own projects.

The analysis helped CARE pinpoint the attributes that led to the successful outcomes in the 15 most effective and efficient projects. For example, high-impact projects included both sanitation and water supply, involved the community heavily in identifying the need for improved systems, delivered health education along with infrastruc-

---

- Does the community have a safe, reliable source of water five years after project completion?
- Is the water system still maintained regularly?
- Do fees from the system's users still cover the cost of maintenance and operations?
- Has the incidence of diarrhea been reduced compared to the rates before the system was built?
- Have the water and sanitation practices covered in health education been maintained?
- Has the watershed been maintained?

Exhibit 5-2   CARE used an *internal* benchmarking process to capture critical success factors in its best projects.

ture, and included community contributions to the construction and maintenance costs as well as the actual construction and maintenance effort. These findings enabled CARE to develop design criteria for future water projects, significantly increasing the chances of sustained impact. They also provided data to justify project funding. At a later stage, this process was combined with regional meetings, where a new water-sector coordinator worked with the water project managers to get a joint definition of best-practice criteria.

Though the benchmarking process uncovered vitally important information for improved performance, CARE's first benchmarking approach—the top-down, headquarters-based method—also provoked considerable resistance. The second approach, with joint headquarters and field development of criteria, followed by project manager self-ranking and improvement plans, was more easily accepted.

One regional meeting using the top-down method provoked intense reactions from the field staff. When the deficiencies of some projects were showcased alongside the strengths of others, some staff objected strongly to a headquarters-imposed process that publicly compared colleagues' performance. The headquarters analysts tried to bring an appropriate even-handedness to the work, and had the benefit of studying multiple projects in order to deduce important success factors, but the effort required better field-staff cooperation. Headquarters staff could not afford to alienate field staff: local knowledge of projects, ability to collect data, and commitment to implement change strategies were essential. (Since country officers raise most of their own project funds, moreover, they are not beholden to headquarters staff, and could have undermined the process.) So while Xerox counts on competition to motivate its employees in reaching new benchmarks, the competitive subtext of top-down benchmarking was anathema to CARE's culture.

Lindenberg noted other challenges to benchmarking:

- Some staff resisted the application of what they saw as a profit-enhancing technique into their mission-oriented work.
- The benchmarks created an imperative for change, which in turn created stress and anxiety as people were required to try new approaches.

- Managing resistance to change
- Finding a balance between internal involvement and outside expertise
- Avoiding cookie-cutter approaches
- Managing suspicion of private sector techniques
- Understanding the difficulties in projecting the benefits of change
- Getting cost information and finding appropriate comparisons
- Comparing costs and benefits across sectors

Exhibit 5-3 CARE USA's experience suggests that nonprofits face additional challenges in benchmarking.

- Benchmarking required considerable investment of time and money.
- Performance indicators were often difficult to establish, especially on complex projects.
- Best practices can vary according to region; they cannot be imposed through a cookie-cutter approach.

Despite the cost and rocky start, CARE remains committed to learning and project quality improvement, and continues to search for strategies that will fit in its culture. (See Exhibit 5-3 for more on cultural adaptation at CARE.) According to Lindenberg, the most successful new efforts involve joint definition of best practices through the participation of project managers, headquarters staff, technicians, and outside experts. Regional line management is taking a larger role in coordinating and overseeing senior-country teams' efforts at quality improvement. Instead of launching learning and change in one movement, CARE decided to sponsor more regional lessons-learned seminars with project managers, followed later by lessons-applied seminars. Additionally, CARE has organized four courses for senior managers, where people from all divisions and regions join together to learn strategic management concepts and frameworks, including how to use benchmarking techniques.

THE BOSTON BALLET

Is benchmarking useful only for companies like Xerox, that can rely on the bottom line for guidance in identifying problems, or for large nonprofits like CARE, that specialize in infrastructure and health projects with fairly evident performance indicators? The Boston Ballet's benchmarking experience suggests that although an outcome like the quality of an artistic performance is impossible to quantify, other aspects of organizational performance can be benchmarked. The Ballet learned that smaller organizations can adapt benchmarking to suit their budgets and culture.

Although it has received national acclaim for its artistic quality and is considered on a par with other major ballet companies, the Boston Ballet felt it lagged behind comparable companies in its ability to raise funds. It also worried that its profile among cultural institutions in Boston was too weak to support a major expansion of its audience and fundraising. With a relatively short 32-year history, it felt dwarfed by local giants like the Boston Symphony Orchestra and the Museum of Fine Arts (both more than 100 years old). So in 1994 it set out on a benchmarking process aimed at enhancing its public image.

The Ballet's board chairman, John Humphrey of The Forum Corporation, led the benchmarking effort by establishing an *ad hoc* committee of both trustees and executive staff. The committee considered several questions as targets for the benchmarking effort before settling on "How do other organizations manage or change their public image?" The question appealed to the committee because it related to the Ballet's goal of enhancing revenues, was broad enough to encompass a number of best practices, and was generic enough to allow the committee to look for best practices in different industries.

In fact, the Ballet ended up turning to a mix of best-practice organizations. Within its field, it chose the San Francisco Ballet, a company with which the Boston Ballet was often compared, and which shared some historical parallels. Looking at another ballet company also offered insights into artistic quality and public image. The Ballet also chose the Boston Museum of Science, which had improved its image in recent years, and Au Bon Pain, a fast growing Boston-based coffee/bakery chain with a reputation for good customer service.

The Ballet's benchmarking process was trustee-driven. The committee developed a questionnaire for use in interviews that they conducted with executives and trustees of the three best-practice organizations. They then summarized the results of the interviews and made recommendations to the board. The process was extremely effective in engaging the Ballet's trustees in a thoughtful exploration of the challenges they faced. Beginning with the development of the interview questions, they explored in depth the processes and programs of the Ballet, including many topics not directly related to image. Traveling in teams to the other organizations and comparing and deliberating findings energized the trustees and tapped their talents. As one board officer remarked, the increased involvement of the trustees was in itself enough of an outcome to justify the effort.

As with all successful benchmarking, the process uncovered specific methods that helped the best-practice organizations achieve success. The Ballet learned, for example, that in organizations with a good image, people can describe the organization's purpose with a simple statement; everyone in the organization delivers the same message about mission, goals, and strategies; there is consistent print image; and customer service and fulfilling promises are high priorities. These findings, which may seem generic and abstract on the written page, were compelling to the benchmarking team who had seen them in action. They saw not only best practices at the other organizations, but also the potential of those practices to help them meet the goals they had set for improving the Ballet's performance.

The benchmarking process also helped trustees understand other issues beyond public image. For example, as trustee Melinda Rabb commented, "The process helped to clarify a new relationship between different worlds that have to exist together—the need to pay homage to the past, yet appeal to new audiences. We kept hearing "world class" and "neighborhood" in the same paragraph."

The benchmarking committee concluded its work by developing recommendations aimed at engaging people throughout the organization in the work of consistent image-building. Recommendations addressed internal education and external publicity; customer responsiveness; and increased efforts to link the Ballet to its local communities. While not all the recommendations have been implemented, work got underway quickly. A major Boston public relations firm, working *pro bono*, created a comprehensive image campaign for the Ballet.

Like Xerox and CARE, the Ballet has concluded that benchmarking can be a useful tool in addressing a number of challenges. The staff discovered other issues that were ripe for benchmarking and began to see the potential value of drawing on outside resources, such as data available from industry groups, to use in the process. For example, when it came to artistic director Bruce Marks' attention that workers' compensation payments (for injuries) swallowed up more than 6 percent of the entire Ballet budget, he concluded that they should consider studying best-practice organizations with a much lower rate of injury. The injury rate was not just a matter of suffering, productivity, or cost. Marks saw in the injury rate some potentially troubling signals about the Ballet's artistic preferences. Its dancers are not "industrial workers," he noted, and the Ballet should "produce people who can do something besides leap over your head." The organization has also challenged itself to engage staff below the senior executive level in the use of benchmarking, a necessary condition, the senior staff feels, for benchmarking to result in improved performance.

WHY BENCHMARKING?

Why invest considerable time and resources in benchmarking, particularly in the cash-strapped nonprofit world? Because nonprofits must maximize the value of what they do with the resources they use. Value, of course, can be defined in many ways by different constituents—including funders, boards, clients, and employees. A learning process like benchmarking enables them to measure *and improve* value. It can provide information for trustees and funders, not only to satisfy their interest in the accomplishment of the mission but also to allow them to execute appropriate oversight. More importantly for most nonprofit professionals, a process like benchmarking enables them to increase the organization's problem-solving capacity. It allows for corrections and improvement in services that can increase effectiveness and impact. Organizational learning can also help in reducing the cost of existing services, freeing up resources to produce more services, which again serves the interests of both funders and clients. (See Exhibit 5-4.)

Without Benchmarking	With Benchmarking
Defining customer requirements	
Based on history or gut feel	Straight reality
Perception	Objective evaluation
Low fit	High conformance
Establishing effective goals and objectives	
Lacking external focus	Credible, unarguable
Reactive	Proactive
Lagging industry	Industry leading
Developing true measures of productivity	
Pursuing pet projects	Solving real problems
Strengths and weaknesses not understood	Understanding outputs
Route of least resistance	Based on industry best practices
Becoming competitive	
Internally focused	Concrete understanding of competition
Evolutionary change	New ideas of proven practices and technology
Low commitment	High commitment
Industry best practices	
Not invented here	Proactive search for change
Few solutions	Many options
Average of industry progress	Business practice breakthrough
Frantic catch-up activity	Superior performance

Source: Robert C. Camp, *Benchmarking: The Search for Industry Best Practices that Lead to Superior Performance*. (Milwaukee: Quality Press, 1989.) Used with permission.

Exhibit 5–4   Key reasons for benchmarking and contrasting results.

> *Value can be defined in many different ways by many different constituents. But funders, clients, and employees will measure value—implicitly, if not explicitly.*

Yet benchmarking is difficult to implement in the nonprofit world, even for managers who understand its value. Benchmarking raises several questions about nonprofit practice and culture:

- Isn't benchmarking a profit-maximizing, competitive weapon, and therefore inconsistent with a mission-driven nonprofit?
- Will the nonprofit service culture resist the analysis and learning that benchmarking requires?
- When managers are overburdened, staffs don't like comparisons, funders don't value overhead, and customers lack market mechanisms, who will drive benchmarking?
- Can small nonprofits afford and benefit from benchmarking?

Answering these questions requires a fuller exploration of benchmarking practices and potential opportunities.

A Tactic for Competitive Advantage or a Tool for Fulfilling a Mission?

To a nonprofit, benchmarking might seem like nothing but a tactic for gaining competitive advantage and maximizing profits. In a sector committed to cooperative traditions, it will take some work to help staff discover that benchmarking is ultimately a value-neutral tool that nonprofits can use to help them fulfill their missions, without compromising their values. Xerox, CARE, and the Boston Ballet had very different goals and missions—profitability, better health in developing countries, and exposing more people to the art of dance—but all used benchmarking to get the outcomes they sought. And they structured the process to fit the culture of their organizations.

It is not necessarily productive, in any case, to hide from the reality that nonprofits are in fact engaged in various forms of competition. They compete for funding, but also for staff, volunteers, and sometimes even clients. If benchmarking allows them to improve their performance and outcomes, it *will* end up giving them competitive advantage. In fact, both CARE and the Ballet were motivated at least in part by the demands of funders or clients to improve their performance. In a resource-scarce world, rewarding the organizations that perform better can be healthy. Ultimately, it is their clients and staff that will benefit from the improved performance.

Even as they compete for resources, many nonprofits simultaneously value cooperation in their work. Their commitment to cooperation can actually improve their ability to use benchmarking effectively. Nonprofit organizations often freely share ideas and collaborate in an effort to advance their shared agendas. This tradition makes benchmarking much more feasible for nonprofits than for many businesses. Nonprofits will be more likely to provide access to an organization engaged in benchmarking than, for example, Chrysler would be to share with GM. Smaller nonprofits (as we discuss further) can share the costs of technical assistance through joint training about benchmarking methods. And within the nonprofit itself, the common tradition of cooperative, team-based work also supports effective benchmarking. A team that clarifies its performance goals, engages in learning together, and formulates implementation strategies will be much better positioned to achieve real improvements within the organization. Teams generate more ideas but also more momentum—both critical if benchmarking is to produce results.

Organizations can use benchmarking to reach their goals, even when that requires balancing competitive and cooperative behaviors. There is nothing inherently profit-maximizing or competitive about the process.

High Performance at the Expense of a Commitment to Service?

Many nonprofits may find their service culture at odds with a learning approach like benchmarking. As a process for analyzing performance, benchmarking emphasizes measuring results, comparing different methods that could improve results, and designing strategies to implement them. At nonprofits like CARE, with a "just-do-it culture," people have little interest in or patience for analysis. In order to engage these committed staff in this kind of process, managers need to introduce techniques that do have the potential to add value by actually improving the services they deliver. The analysis and innovation that benchmarking can generate are wholly consistent with their ultimate goal of service: doing public good.

Improving the service rendered, or making a nonprofit more efficient so it can serve more people, is an integral part of realizing a service mission.

Why do the staff at service-oriented organizations often resist the analysis and measurement required by benchmarking? Although many organizations rely on specialized or professional skills, nonprofit workers often view their work more as art than science. Many feel (probably rightly) that every combination of circumstance, program, and professional effort is unique, and (probably wrongly) that analyzing and comparing them at any level is impossible. Nonprofit workers also tend to place a premium on shared values, mutual respect, and professional esteem, and would be reluctant to make comparisons even if they could. They believe it demeans the contributions of people or organizations.[1] And many employees are ultimately committed to providing service to the individuals they work with. They see organizational analysis as a diversion from, not an enhancement of, their service work.

This culture has led to organizational systems and structures—even the informal practices of small nonprofits—that were established to get the job done, not to rethink the nature of the job, or the possibilities for improving performance. Effective organizational learning, moreover, takes the kind of discipline and resource investment that doesn't necessarily pay off in the short term and thus doesn't emerge as a top priority in most nonprofits. Faced with the choice of doing or analyzing, most nonprofits opt for doing, and avoid the challenge of establishing performance metrics. As a result, few nonprofits have the data and information needed to "know yourself," the first step in Warren Jeffries' playbook at Xerox.

> *Faced with the choice of doing or analyzing, most nonprofits opt for doing.*

Here nonprofits encounter another problem: Many have difficulty defining and measuring the outcomes of their work. This does not mean, though, that they cannot improve their performance through benchmarking. Even while they tackle the challenge of defining outcomes and metrics for their programs, nonprofits can begin to use benchmarking on the *procedures* they are currently using to achieve results. The Boston Ballet's mission of promoting appreciation for the art of dance is difficult to measure. But the Ballet's benchmarking process focused on how its communications process affected its image, and thereby its funding and audience size. Businesses have only recently begun documenting process flows, which would illuminate in the Ballet's case the linkage between communications, image, and audience. Most nonprofits have never allocated the skills and time needed for this type of documentation. But it offers potentially large payoffs as part of a learning process, and can enable nonprofits to improve their methods.

Who Will Provide the Momentum for Benchmarking?

Benchmarking brings into sharp focus some of the common obstacles that nonprofits face in building support for organizational capacity. Unlike some other management processes (e.g., human resources or program development), benchmarking is largely an optional strategy for most organizations. Because they do not need to use benchmarking, building support for it becomes all the more difficult. No one will force nonprofits to benchmark, and no one is likely to reward them quickly if they do. Unlike a company like Xerox, most nonprofits will not feel consumer pressure to measure and improve performance: nonprofit clients often lack a choice in providers. Nonprofit boards, another possible champion of a performance-improving process like benchmarking, too often draw a sharp line between policy and management, and view benchmarking as a staff matter. Finally, even when funders do require performance data, it may not help an organization with benchmarking. They are likely to want data on outcomes—not the processes that produced them.

As a result, the burden of developing a compelling case for benchmarking falls to the leaders of a nonprofit. They must be willing to risk exposing their organizations' strengths and weaknesses and be willing to make a commitment to improvement. Nonprofit managers and boards will have to define their organizational-learning needs, design compelling and feasible approaches to them, and present their case to funders and staff.

A Benefit to Small Organizations

Size need not determine managerial sophistication and competence. Size can play a major role in the availability of resources and expertise, however, particularly in the nonprofit domain. A leader in a small nonprofit needs not only knowledge, but access to a tool before she can apply that resource in an organization. Both of the nonprofit organizations profiled in this chapter stressed the level of commitment needed to undertake benchmarking in the face of limited resources for surveys and analytical work.

Small nonprofits need not rule out benchmarking as a tool for improving performance. They can turn the sector's cooperative tradition to their advantage by collaborating with each other or teaming with more experienced sponsoring organizations on benchmarking. For example, many small nonprofits are members of national or regional groups that produce conferences, coordinate site visits, and promote interorganizational learning. Some of that energy could support development of active, performance-oriented benchmarking processes. Eureka Communities, a Washington, D.C.-based nonprofit that serves small, community-based organizations, funds and coordinates study trips to enable nonprofit managers to study best practices up close—an ingenious response to the needs of small nonprofits. Larger national intermediaries and membership organizations could consider similar programs, and make the tool available to smaller nonprofits.

> *Smaller nonprofits can turn the sector's cooperative tradition to their advantage by collaborating with each other or teaming with more experienced sponsoring organizations.*

CONCLUSION

The benchmarking process can give nonprofits the information, ideas, and strategies they need to improve their performance. The process works, as CARE and the Boston Ballet discovered, but only when an organization is motivated enough to take on this intensive, active style of learning. Nonprofits themselves will have to cultivate that motivation. But if they discover that improving performance directly advances their mission, they will find themselves able to overcome the obstacles and challenges involved in benchmarking, and achieving better outcomes as a result.

ORGANIZATION PROFILES

Xerox

800 Long Ridge Road, Stamford, CT 06904; www.xerox.com

Founded: 1906, as The Haloid Company, a producer of photographic paper

Core business: Document processing products and systems

Scope: Thousands of divisions and sales offices worldwide; 91,400 employees; $18.2 billion revenue (1997)

Key benchmarking lessons:

- Begin with self-knowledge—an understanding of strengths and weaknesses.
- Focus on learning and planning, then doing.
- Look at processes, not just products.
- Learn from (and compare yourself to) the best, regardless of industry.
- The real benefit of benchmarking comes from understanding the business practices that underlie benchmarked performance.

CARE USA

151 Ellis Street, Atlanta, GA 30303; www.care.org

Founded: 1945, now part of an 11-organization world confederation

Core business: International relief, rehabilitation, and sustainable development

Scope: Projects and offices in 37 countries; 9,000 employees; $359 million budget (1996)

Key benchmarking lessons:

- Use internal comparisons if external comparisons are not possible.
- Concentrate initially on areas of strength.
- Prepare for organizational stress—particularly by involving people throughout the organization.
- Use nonprofit culture as an advantage by promoting cooperation.

Boston Ballet

19 Clarendon Street, Boston, MA 02116-6100; www.boston.com/bostonballet

Founded: 1963, with a grant from the Ford Foundation and artistic assistance from George Balanchine

Core business: Promoting dance

Scope: 43 dancers; 14,000+ subscribers; 242,000 patrons annually; 400+ volunteers; $16 million budget (1997)

Key benchmarking lessons:

- Don't wait for a crisis to begin learning.
- Involve board, management, staff, and other stakeholders.
- The learning process may be as important as the outcomes.
- Pay attention to other issues that arise during the benchmarking process.

ADDITIONAL READING

Camp, Robert C. *Benchmarking—The Search for Industries' Best Practices that Lead to Superior Performance.* Milwaukee, WI: ASQC Quality Press, 1989.

Camp, Robert C. *Business Process Benchmarking: Finding and Implementing Best Practices.* Milwaukee: ASQC Quality Press, 1995.

Kaplan, Robert S. and David P. Norton. *The Balanced Scorecard: Translating Strategy Into Action.* Boston, MA: Harvard Business School Press, 1996.

Martin, Lawrence L. and Peter M. Kettner. *Measuring the Performance of Human Service Programs.* Thousand Oaks, CA: Sage Publications, 1996.

National Performance Review. *From Red Tape to Results: Creating a Government that Works Better & Costs Less.* Washington, DC: General Printing Office, 1993.

Watson, Gregory H. *Strategic Benchmarking.* New York: John Wiley & Sons, 1995.

ENDNOTE

[1]For more on this, see Chapter 6.

CHAPTER SIX

Human Resources: Developing Employees to Advance Organizational Goals

FRAMING QUESTIONS

▶ How can organizations "invest in people" when facing financial constraints and high staff turnover?

▶ What's at the root of so many burnout problems in the nonprofit world?

▶ How can strategic HR help organizations deliver on their mission?

Nonprofit employees and volunteers embody the distinctive essence of the nonprofit sector: They are deeply committed to the social causes their organizations address and are inspired by the possibility of "making a difference." Thanks to this asset, the human resources challenge facing nonprofits is different from that of most for-profits. Their biggest challenge is not to *attract* motivated people—they will seek out nonprofit opportunities—but to channel their energy so it advances the organization's mission and goals. Although this alignment of the sector's motivated people and its organizational goals has profound potential, many nonprofits are focusing instead on the very human resources problems, including low pay, short career ladders, and the overwork that contribute to burnout, that they feel powerless to solve. Few may realize that the most sophisticated human resources (HR) strategies are actually within the reach of most nonprofits, and could improve their prospects for achieving real social impact. To get new results from more strategic HR practices, though, nonprofits will have to fundamentally rethink what HR is and what it can do for them.

The most important shift is to see HR practices as strategic: They aim not just to provide jobs for people committed to public service, but rather to get, keep, and motivate good people *specifically to advance the objectives and mission of the organization.* Conventional HR views these challenges in isolation, and ends up with a vague and daunting challenge: "How can we get good people and keep them happy?" But by linking recruiting, retention, and motivation to organizational objectives, strategic HR addresses the needs of the client, the organization, and its employees simultaneously. With this approach, managers do not face a job to get done on the one hand and an employee to keep happy on the other. Organizing jobs so employees can achieve and see results does both: It advances the organization's mission and motivates people in the process.

COMMON NONPROFIT RESPONSES TO HUMAN RESOURCES

The shift toward strategic HR is an enormous one for any organization, perhaps particularly for nonprofits. Some of the most common nonprofit approaches focus on compensation policies, administration, and training. All of these practices are important in their own right, but none is an effective substitute for strategic HR.

Many nonprofits, for example, may conclude that the only HR issue that counts is compensation (or other benefits that only money can buy) and that, because funds are so limited, there is little they can do to improve their situations.[1] But as many businesses have learned, good salaries may be important in recruiting, and important in helping to prevent *dissatisfaction*, but are of little use in motivating employees and supporting performance. As influential research by psychologist Frederick Herzberg showed 30 years ago,[2] *achieving results* is what motivates people. This is a critical distinction for nonprofit human resources management.

Other nonprofits are focusing on improving the administrative aspects of human resources. For example, they are teaching managers how to develop better recordkeeping and performance evaluation systems, or codifying personnel policies in manuals. Meanwhile, the trend in business is to outsource (e.g., recordkeeping) or eliminate (e.g., formal evaluations) these functions as companies increasingly reconceive of HR as a matter of organizational strategy that all managers are involved with.[3]

The Independent Sector, the leading voice of the nonprofit sector, reflects these views of human resources in its 1996 report on future leadership.[4] The report makes a compelling case for the nonprofit sector to develop an administrative and compensation agenda, focusing on salaries, benefits, and performance evaluations. It also urges inclusiveness in hiring to create a more diverse workplace. But it gives very little attention to the nature of nonprofit jobs, and how they contribute to the development of satisfying, productive nonprofit careers, not to mention the advancement of nonprofits' goals and objectives.

In some respects, the nonprofit sector has been a leader in recruiting and human-capital strategies. "Leadership development" is popular, especially for community-based organizations that rely on the talents of volunteer, often untrained workers to succeed. Fellowships and internships are offered to attract talented young people to nonprofits. Some funders offer support and recognition for "social entrepreneurs." Many of the professions active in nonprofits offer their own training and learning opportunities. These strategies can help individuals improve their personal capacities, but they are not enough to help organizations improve their capacity for performance.

REDEFINING HUMAN RESOURCES AS A STRATEGY FOR DELIVERING ON MISSION

High performing organizations have created ways to support, challenge, equip, and develop their staffs, all in the context of refining and meeting the organization's mission. In our inquiry, we uncovered several cases that illustrate the potential and difficulty of using human resources to serve employees and their organizations.

In high performing organizations, meeting the minimal requirements of "good jobs at fair wages" does not suffice.

HEWLETT-PACKARD

The high-tech electronics giant Hewlett-Packard's human resources strategies are legendary in the business world. Hewlett-Packard's approach is straightforward: to make the company "the best place to work." From the employee end, that sounds very appealing. What makes this strategy extraordinary is the view from the investor's perspective: Hewlett-Packard returned an average $458 in 1997 for each hundred dollars invested in 1992—compared to $403 for similar companies and $247 for the general market. Not coincidentally, one of the best places to work is also one of the best places to invest.

Robin Purcell, human resources manager for the Medical Products Group of Hewlett-Packard, describes how this strategy works in her 4,600-employee, $1.4 billion-revenue division. The "HP Way," she explains, starts with the belief that "people are our only sustainable competitive advantage." (See Exhibit 6-1.) HR is the key to sustaining that resource.

Hewlett-Packard does not protect employees from hard work and intense pressure to create successful new products, or from the heightened pressure for productivity produced by global competi-

MBWA = Management by Wandering Around
TQC = Total Quality Management
MBO = Management by Objective

The "HP Way" is the foundation for Hewlett-Packard's corporate culture. Enduring Organizational Values are at the core, while Corporate Objectives guide decision-making. Strategies and Practices change in response to external and internal business conditions, but they remain consistent with the company's Organizational Values and Corporate Objectives.

Source: Reproduced with permission of Hewlett-Packard Company.

Exhibit 6-1 "People are our only sustainable competitive advantage." Hewlett-Packard's "HP Way" puts values—shared and sustained through strategic human resources investment—at the core of its corporate strategy.

tion. Purcell claims that a typical employee, asked to describe what makes Hewlett-Packard a great place to work, might say: "I work with people who I am challenged by, who I enjoy working with. We're working on neat stuff. And for the most part it's an enjoyable work environment, in spite of all the stress of what we're trying to accomplish and the time frames we're trying to accomplish it in."

Under these competitive conditions, Hewlett-Packard needs to ensure that its employees can maximize their abilities. Its strategy focuses on supporting workers, developing them, challenging them, giving them the tools they need and holding them accountable for results. Hewlett-Packard has always regarded this challenge as the business of every manager, not the province of a few specialists. It's significant that the company had no human resources department at all for its first 18 years, and did not put a personnel professional in the top HR post until 1989, by which time the integration of HR into the culture had been firmly established. Hewlett-Packard is consciously trying to lower the ratio of human resources professionals to employees, and toward that end has begun outsourcing all HR administrative functions so it can concentrate on helping managers create and maintain a performance-focused environment. The company's approach raises several themes:

- *Loyalty to the employee.* In return for performance, Hewlett-Packard obligates itself to its employees with loyalty. The company asks employees, "How can you affect the success and the health of our business?" In turn, it offers loyalty and opportunities for personal growth and development.[5] Hewlett-Packard's "no layoff" objective (amended recently to "job security based on performance") links performance and loyalty overtly. As an alternative to layoffs, employees receive help finding a job elsewhere within the company. As a last resort, Hewlett-Packard will *guarantee* them a job, perhaps less desirable or in a different location, but will preserve their salary for up to three years. If employees choose to leave, they get a generous severance package, based on length of service. In return for this commitment, Hewlett-Packard wants workers to understand the company's objectives and situation so they can support its success actively.

- *Challenging workers, even when career ladders are shorter.* While Hewlett-Packard's revenues have continued to grow, the number of employees has grown at a much slower rate. With fewer higher-level positions available, managers cannot reward people with promotions on the traditional career ladder. Instead, Purcell says, Hewlett-Packard looks for other "ways to keep people challenged and excited—by making lateral moves, by assigning them to high-visibility task teams, by having them look at a particular business problem, and having them participate on corporate task forces. We are much more willing to get people out of their own day-to-day box, and that has the value of building new skills, building visibility and keeping people challenged and excited in a work environment."

> *"We are much more willing to get people out of their own day-to-day box, and that has the value of building new skills, building visibility and keeping people challenged and excited in a work environment."*

- *Evaluating performance in terms of results and attitude.* Performance evaluations not only consider skills and achievements, but also the attitude of workers. "It's not just, 'Did you get the results?' It's also 'How did you get the results?' And the 'how' includes, 'Are you bringing others along? Are you leaving a nasty wake when you achieve your results? . . . If you're really working but not getting the results, but you've got all the other attributes, we'll work with you. Not forever, but we'll work.'"
- *Rewarding performance with bonuses.* Compensation policies at Hewlett-Packard reward excellence: Salaries for the same job can differ by up to 50 percent based on performance.
- *Using data to develop effective HR policy.* HR professionals closely track trends on topics like minority recruitment and retention of female managers. The Medical Products Group, disturbed that it is losing good senior-level professional women, is con-

ducting research, including focus groups, exit interviews, and post-exit tracking, to see where women go after leaving the company, to help managers retain these employees.

GREATER BOSTON REHABILITATION SERVICES

What if you're not a multinational electronics giant? What if, instead, you're a struggling nonprofit human-service organization facing extinction in a rapidly changing funding marketplace? This was the situation Terry Ann Lunt faced when she assumed the director's post at Greater Boston Rehabilitation Services (GBRS) in 1991. Her HR strategies show how sophisticated practices similar to Hewlett-Packard's, but appropriate for a small nonprofit, can deliver results without expensive processes or outside experts.

Founded in 1961 with no government money and all volunteers, GBRS offers three services. First, it provides vocational rehabilitation services to disabled people (most with mental illness) via a sheltered workshop. GBRS offers "real jobs for real wages," but with the pace and demands of work adapted for the special needs of disabled people. Second, it helps sheltered workshop participants find permanent jobs in mainstream workplaces once they have the necessary skills and capacities. Third, it provides contract services to private companies, including production work that GBRS completes at the companies' facilities.

GBRS had three major sites, employing over 200 workers in light assembly and packaging for several clients, including Polaroid Corporation and Lotus Development Corporation. Its staff included: eight rehabilitation counselors (with undergraduate and graduate degrees) who were supervised by a psychologist and a consulting psychiatrist; a financial officer (with a bachelor's degree in marketing); a production manager (a retired firefighter) who ran the workshop; and four employment counselors (all social-service workers with no previous employment training or placement experience). Lunt says GBRS had the "culture of a small family business."

After a short period of growth pushed revenues from $200,000 to $3.5 million per year, changing markets threatened the very survival of GBRS. Cash from funders and work assignments from contract clients fell off. The state was beginning to favor job placement for disabled people in regular workplaces in the community, and had reduced significantly two large contracts for GBRS's sheltered work as part of this policy change. Lotus, a major client, was shifting to "just-in-time" processes. A standing group of GBRS workers would not accommodate the new production schedules, which would fluctuate with consumer demand. Lotus was considering using a temporary-work agency for the flexibility they would need. At the same time, a capital campaign consultant retained earlier by GBRS delivered bad news: Although they had been in the community for 30 years, "no one knew what we did," and there was little chance a campaign would succeed.

While all organizations have to navigate treacherous changes, Lunt worried that GBRS seemed especially ill-equipped. "The organization really had no infrastructure. There was no HR-personnel function. There were no information systems. There were no budgets or financial reporting systems or routines. There was no development or fundraising. There was no communications or marketing. No planning process. Nothing."

Although GBRS's plight was a function of all these problems, strategic human resources management became the key to stabilizing the organization. Finding the people who could get the results needed, restructuring jobs to help them succeed, and measuring and rewarding performance helped the organization address its most critical challenges.

> *Finding the people who could get the results needed, restructuring jobs to help them succeed, and measuring and rewarding performance helped the organization address its most critical challenges.*

Lunt's response illustrates a strategic approach to HR. First, she began hiring people whose skills and outlook would help the organization perform its core work and, not coincidentally, begin to change the culture. Specifically, GBRS needed new people who could increase the organization's success in placing its clients in jobs. "We had workers who were in social services to help disabled people, not to make cold calls, and we needed people who could sell our candidates' abilities, not their disabilities." This shift required Lunt to look more for skill sets (particularly in sales and marketing) to support specific goals, and less for professions (like social work) that fit the broader mission. As part of her strategy, Lunt recruited "refugees" from the corporate world who wanted to "make a difference" but were also attracted to the opportunity of working on organizational challenges.

Second, she began restructuring jobs to get the most out of the small staff. She "pulled apart jobs and rebundled them" to create work that made the best use of people's skills and satisfied their interests. She instituted a team-work approach to help people draw on each other's strengths. She hired two talented women who wanted challenging, but not full-time work (both had young children), and created a job-share to accommodate them.

Third, to motivate the staff, Lunt focused on creating jobs that would both challenge workers and demand high performance. She emphasized the importance of measuring the success of their efforts, so that employees could see and enjoy the results of their work. Clear work plans and goals helped employees focus on performance. Employees who could not perform were encouraged to leave.

Fourth, GBRS instituted new compensation policies to ensure that dissatisfaction over pay did not undermine other efforts to sustain motivation. She paid above the norm (sometimes up to 20 percent), noting that "you always have choices about how you spend your money." Toward the end of her tenure, she began experimenting with performance-based pay. If people attained 80 percent of the goals they had set earlier in consultation with their managers, they would get a raise (determined by the amount of money available).

Finally, GBRS looked for other ways to acknowledge and support its employees' best efforts. It regularly praised and recognized people for their success by attracting media attention to their achievements, nominating employees for professional awards, and soliciting client feedback so employees would know how their work was valued. The organization also moved out of its "small, dumpy, ugly space for way too much money" into more appealing quarters.

Over the next few years, GBRS saw:

- Job placement increase over 300 percent
- Staff turnover largely eliminated
- Its first grants from local and national foundations (for innovative programs designed by GBRS staff)
- Its contract with Lotus not only continued, but made exclusive for daytime shifts
- A GBRS staff-created curriculum adapted by Lotus for Lotus's own employees
- More than 20 long-term clients moved into competitive employment
- An increase in state contracts[6]

PUBLIC ALLIES

Public Allies is an example of a nonprofit at an earlier point in its life. On the cusp between a youthful growth spurt and institutionalization, it discovered why an organization needs a capacity for strategic HR, and how to begin building it.

Vanessa Kirsch and Katrina Brown co-founded Public Allies in 1991 as a direct response to the obstacles facing young people starting out in the nonprofit sector. A survey Kirsch had done with Peter Hart Research revealed that young people felt isolated from opportunities to make a difference. Further research from the Advocacy Institute underscored the problems young people faced in taking entry-level nonprofit jobs: burnout, short career ladders, low pay, and lack of professional development opportunities. Public Allies wanted to help young people find jobs in the nonprofit sector; help them develop career paths; and, in the process, help community-based nonprofits reap the benefits of their talents.

To meet these goals, Public Allies began recruiting on behalf of the community-based nonprofits. It looked for young people with leadership potential in neighborhoods, through door-to-door canvassing, at youth centers, and on college campuses. Those selected for the program (the "Allies") were placed in ten-month apprenticeships at nonprofit organizations in their communities. The apprenticeships were structured to help the Allies develop their skills. Public Allies provided extensive and ongoing support to the apprentices, including one day a week of special training, informal coaching, and help in developing career plans.

The idea resonated with funders, and Public Allies quickly headed into a steep growth curve, developing within five years from a $250,000- to a $3-million operation with 30 staff in one central and six local offices. But as Kirsch and her colleagues managed their blossoming project, they discovered their own organizational challenges in human resources management. "Though we were trying to encourage nonprofit organizations to value their young people as human resources," says Kirsch, "it was incredibly hard to create the systems to do it ourselves."

Kirsch and her senior managers identified two major challenges to ensuring that people within their own organization had meaningful work where their performance would matter. First, the diverse, highly motivated, and entrepreneurial staff wanted interesting, challenging, and well-supported jobs. This was especially so for those whom Kirsch recruited from the private sector. They were willing to accept lower-paying jobs, but only in return for "interesting work." Second, it was difficult to use results as a motivator when those results were hard to measure. Like many nonprofits focused on human development, Public Allies found it difficult to quantify short-term outcomes. It was looking for results for its Allies five years out, not at what happened in their lives in a given week. It was also difficult to assess staff performance. The line between truly external forces and individual performance was a blurry one.

Meanwhile, the organization's growth compounded its HR challenges. At a small scale, human resources support was provided informally or as needed. But as job assignments became more specialized, older staff members joined, and time horizons for planning grew longer, an informal HR approach seemed inadequate. "An emphasis on human resources means you're no longer entrepreneurial," Kirsch says. "You've begun to institutionalize."

Added to these challenges were other realities of nonprofit life: Managers have little time or support to develop human resources (or any other organizational) strategies. "Recruiting and sustaining talent at Public Allies was one of the largest and most time-consuming parts of the job for me," Kirsch notes. Yet as every executive of a young nonprofit discovers, she was forced to devote a huge share of her time to fundraising and the development of new sites. Most of the money raised, moreover, could not be used for the development of internal HR strategies. Funders offered grants for growth, evaluation, or program improvement, but little to support the capacity of the organization to manage all those functions. After a dogged effort, however, the Kellogg Foundation offered Public Allies what Kirsch calls "the ideal grant": $1.4 million to help them "develop the human potential of our organization" by building organizational systems and capacity.

Public Allies has used the Kellogg funding to undertake, among other things, a strategic planning process, and to develop management systems that will support the implementation of the plan. Public Allies will also analyze the success factors of its early years and identify the skills it will need as the organization continues to grow. With this information, it can make its HR more strategic: It can recruit people with these objectives in mind, support them to achieve these objectives, and motivate them with the results they achieve. Meanwhile, Public Allies employees can take satisfaction from the longer-term results now being documented. A recent survey of Public Allies "alumni" found that 95 percent were in school and/or employed, and that 64 percent of those employed worked in the nonprofit sector.

As it continues to grow and address its own HR challenges, Public Allies continues to develop new strategies to help community-based nonprofits and young people with their human resources agendas. For example, it recognized the "stratification" problem of the nonprofit sector—many organizations have a few senior positions and a number of entry-level jobs, and very little in between—as a potential stumbling block for program graduates with skill levels that fell in the middle. So it has created opportunities for young people to "shadow" senior managers at Public Allies, exposing them to the upper end of the career ladder, and a "next-step" program for alumni of the one-year Allies to help them advance their career goals. For its apprentices and the community nonprofits where they work, Public Allies has also begun offering quarterly conferences on organizational development.

These cases put HR in a new, organizational context and raise several key issues for managers, boards, and funders: (1) the value of using HR as a strategy for advancing the organization's mission, (2) the impact of low salaries on strategic HR, and (3) the importance of results-oriented jobs to motivation.

USING STRATEGIC HUMAN RESOURCES TO ADVANCE SOCIAL MISSIONS

All the organizations profiled here understand that effective human resources management is not just about finding and keeping people. It's about finding, keeping, and managing people *in ways that will help the organization meet its goals*. Hewlett-Packard might well attract creative, hard-working employees, but unless they are managed specifically to meet corporate objectives, HR is not fundamentally strategic. By the same token, the staff that Terry Ann Lunt inherited at GBRS were hardly incompetent or unmotivated. Lunt's challenge was to recruit, organize, and support employees to stabilize the organization, particularly by increasing the placement of clients by taking a "sales" approach. Similarly, by defining the skills that supported its early successes and the skills needed for future expansion, Public Allies can now recruit and develop employees to support their goals of program impact and successful expansion.

Effective human resources management is not just about finding and keeping people. It's about finding, keeping, and managing people in ways that will help the organization meet its goals.

As noted, the trend among for-profit human resources professionals is to invest in the strategic aspects of HR. Companies are increasingly outsourcing the administration of payroll and benefits, while insisting that all managers, not just HR specialists, focus on motivating workers and supporting their development. Nonprofits that are now emphasizing the administrative aspects of HR (e.g., better evaluation and tighter personnel policies) may be heading in the wrong direction, particularly if they see HR *only* as a matter of back-office administration. Strategic HR is likely to have much greater value for them, no matter what their size or state of affairs. Nonprofits that think of strategic human resources as an expensive amenity for only the largest, most stable, and best-funded organizations should consider that just the opposite can be true: It can be difficult to survive *without* an ambitious, focused human resources strategy.

Strategic HR takes commitment and analysis more than money or a specialized HR department. Even Hewlett-Packard (with more capital than any nonprofit) has developed HR approaches that reflect fiscal constraints. It uses "special assignments" and "lateral promotions" to offer workers greater challenges and more satisfaction without expanding the ranks of expensive senior managers. GBRS hired two part-time workers and blended their skills in a lower-cost package. Public Allies has focused on recruiting for the skills it has learned it needs, and for the skills expansion will require. All of these moves require insight into the value of strategic HR—and have served nonprofit employees and their goals well.

COMPENSATION: A CRITICAL BUT LIMITED HUMAN RESOURCES TOOL

Taking a strategic approach to HR, however, does not mean nonprofits should not worry about compensation. They should worry about it and deal with it, keeping in mind two important dynamics: (1) low salaries do cause problems for nonprofits, but (2) many nonprofits may be more *unwilling* than *unable* to pay their people better.

No one disputes that poor pay is a problem for many nonprofits, a finding confirmed by the research that inspired Public Allies and a concern noted by the Independent Sector in its call for a new non-profit human resources agenda. Poor pay creates job dissatisfaction, which is then often compounded by the burnout that comes from working for long periods on difficult social problems. But what makes the compensation problem particularly complicated for nonprofits is that many are actually ambivalent about it. They recognize it creates hardship and demoralizes employees, but are unwilling to correct it. As Nora Lester, Melissa Lamson, and Neil Wollman observed in a study of nonprofits devoted to social change, nonprofit employees often "speak as if there is only so much well-being to go around, and any well-being that staff get is deducted directly from the people they serve."[7] Even so, these employees may still experience low pay as a hardship, and it if doesn't leave them discouraged and resentful, it may eventually lead them to seek other career paths.

For people who make an affirmative commitment to personal sacrifice as an essential part of their nonprofit service, low pay is not a problem that needs to be corrected. For example, members of religious orders who take a vow of poverty are not later demoralized by low pay. Other organizations may similarly emphasize service over employment. In its early years, for example, Habitat for Humanity paid its headquarters staff not according to what the market (even the nonprofit market) dictated, but according to what each needed to meet personal and family obligations. But for the many nonprofits where employees view themselves as committed *employees*, not volunteers with stipends, an *implicit* decision to disregard compensation is dangerous.

Nonprofits that understand the importance of decent pay often muster the will to fund it. As Terry Ann Lunt points out, nonprofit managers do "have the choice" to pay better, and should resist the "tyranny of the bottom line," focusing so relentlessly on cost constraints that they fail to make important investments. She could not match private-sector salaries dollar-for-dollar, but she could raise salaries to the point where they were no longer a major impediment in recruiting, and could try creative measures like job-sharing between two working mothers to enhance job appeal. Similarly, in recruiting the best director possible for one of the Public Allies' field offices, Kirsch discovered she had to pay above their normal range, but accepted the cost as an investment in the organization's capacity to perform.

> *Nonprofit managers must beware of the "tyranny of the bottom line," focusing so relentlessly on cost constraints that they fail to make important investments.*

In the end, though, managers need to understand the limitations of good pay. It is more a protection against dissatisfaction than a source of motivation for the long term. Pay cannot substitute for the satisfaction that comes from producing results, which is another vital aspect of strategic HR.

UNDERSTANDING JOBS, RESULTS, AND MOTIVATION

If money is not the key to sustaining motivation and job satisfaction, what is? For many nonprofits, it would seem that the personal commitment of employees is enough. If everyone in the organization is "fighting the good fight" or providing a service they believe to be socially important, why worry? Indeed, many do join an organization because it gives them an opportunity to work for a cause or issue they find compelling. But to stay productive, motivated, and satisfied over the long term, employees need to achieve and see results. Effective HR strategies, therefore, structure jobs that enable employees to do that.

Nothing may be as important in nonprofit HR as linking jobs and results. The problem of burnout, so prevalent among nonprofit employees, is caused not only by difficult work, or even lots of difficult work, but by difficult work that does not seem to produce results. Many nonprofits are devoted to addressing problems that will take years to solve. And as Michael O'Neill, of the Institute for Nonprofit Management, University of San Francisco, observes, few nonprofit employees "can endure low wages and long hours for the ten, twenty, or thirty years that is usually required to make a difference."[8] The problem of results-thin jobs also plagues people new to the sector, who haven't yet spent years trying to tackle difficult issues. Kirsch's survey found that young people were discouraged early in their nonprofit careers because they felt they were not advancing the organization's mission, much less changing society. Nor could they see any career ladder that would offer them more results-generating work in the near term.

It is difficult for many nonprofits to motivate people with results. "When you're in the behavioral change business or human-service field, it's hard to measure results," Alice Howard, principal of Vista Consulting, comments. This was a problem that both Public Allies and GBRS faced. GBRS staff ended up devising their own goals and outcome measures, in addition to those required by funders, because they felt that employees needed to see results they valued. At Public Allies, Kirsch tried to disaggregate the organization's ambitious mission into "bite-sized chunks" that individual staff members or teams could aim to meet. In addition, the organization looked for ways to demonstrate impact, both in the lives of the Allies and in the organizations where they worked. After listening to the GBRS story, one observer expressed her regrets about leaving the nonprofit sector. A manager like Lunt early in her career would have kept her in the sector, she said. As it was, she couldn't see her work leading anywhere. "Good people are often results-oriented people," she concluded.

Developing effective HR strategies is a challenge for any organization. Hewlett-Packard is a hero in the business press precisely because it succeeds at something hard. The company works vigilantly to reinforce the link between "good jobs" and strategic outcomes (see Exhibit 6-2). And what's hard for business is even harder for nonprofit managers, who often have little support or encouragement for pursuing organizational strategies like HR. As Lunt put it, "The culture doesn't value management. It really doesn't understand that you couldn't do what you do without a

---

"Our People" (from a company presentation)

HP's primary sustainable competitive advantage is our ability to create an environment which attracts, develops, and retains highly talented people. HP's leadership position as "the best place to work" cannot be assumed in the future. Technology advancements and global competition are accelerating changes in HP's activities and causing a more stressful work environment worldwide. To remain an employer of choice, we must

- Ensure that all segments of our diverse workforce are fully valued and included.
- Foster and support a philosophy of continuous learning and career self-reliance.
- Help employees manage the increasing demands of work and other life activities consistent with our business needs.
- Create an injury-free work environment.

Exhibit 6–2   Hewlett-Packard reinforces the link between "good jobs" and strategic outcomes.

healthy organization." For this reason, Public Allies, and so many other nonprofits, have struggled to get funding to support management capability.

INVESTING IN HUMAN POTENTIAL

Although it faces daunting HR problems, the nonprofit sector has important resources for overcoming them. Leadership from organizations like Independent Sector, solutions from initiatives like Public Allies', and funding for fellowships, training, and professional development are all promising. What has been missing, but is within the reach of most nonprofits, is an understanding of HR as an organizational process that nonprofits can study and develop. On this front, the potential is enormous. Nonprofits already have the advantage of compelling missions. If they can match those with compelling jobs, they can dramatically improve the prospects for recruiting and developing the best people, not to mention their prospects for delivering on their missions.

ORGANIZATION PROFILES

Hewlett-Packard

3000 Hanover Street, Palo Alto, CA 94304-1185; www.hp.com

Founded: 1937 as a small electronic instrument company

Core business: Electronic products and systems for measurement, computing, and communication

Scope: 600 sales and support offices and distributorships in 120 countries; 122,000 employees; $42.9 billion revenue (1997)

Key HR practices:

- Loyalty to the employee
- Challenging workers despite short career ladders
- Evaluating attitude as well as results
- Rewarding performance
- Analyzing data

"People are our only sustainable competitive advantage."

Greater Boston Rehabilitation Services

34 Monsignor O'Brien Highway, Cambridge, MA 02141

Founded: 1961, as an all-volunteer organization

Core business: Employment opportunities for disabled persons

Scope: Boston-area; 23 employees; $2 million budget (1997)

Key HR practices:

- Hiring to supply core competencies needed for mission fulfillment
- Rebundling jobs to match existing skills
- Challenging workers
- Rewarding performance

"We sell our clients' abilities, not their disabilities."

Public Allies

1015 18th Street, NW, Suite 200, Washington, DC 20036

Founded: 1991, as an independent 501 (c) (3)

Core business: Placing young leaders in nonprofits

Scope: Nationwide; 7 sites; 45 employees; $3.5 million budget (1997)

Key HR practices:

- Extensive support
- Career development assistance
- Challenging work; visible results
- Separating external forces from individual performance issues

ADDITIONAL READING

Beer, Michael. *Managing Human Assets*. New York: The Free Press/ Macmillan, 1984.

Beer, Michael. "The Transformation of the Human Resource Function: Resolving the Tension Between a Traditional Administrative and a New Strategic Role," *Human Resource Management*, Spring 1997, Vol. 36, No. 1.

Herzberg, Frederick. "One More Time: How Do You Motivate Employees?" *Harvard Business Review*, Vol. 65, No. 5, September–October 1987.

Lester, Nora, Melissa Lamson, and Neil Wollman. "How Staff Get Burned (Out) by Social Change Work," *Journal of Community Advocacy and Activism*, Vol. 2, June 1997.

Miller, Lynne E., ed., *Managing Human Service Organizations*. New York: Quorum Books, 1989.

Ulrich, Dave. "A New Mandate for Human Resources," *Harvard Business Review*, January–February 1998, pp. 125–134.

Ulrich, David, Michael R. Losey, and Gerry Lake, eds. *Tomorrow's HR Management: 48 Thought Leaders Call for Change*. New York: John Wiley & Sons, 1997.

ENDNOTES

[1]See, for example: Pablo Eisenberg, "Non-Profit World Must Reach Out to Its Future" in *The Chronicle of Philanthropy*, September 18, 1997; or David La Piana, "Beyond Collaboration: Strategic Restructuring of Nonprofit Organizations" (Los Angeles: James

Irvine Foundation, 1997). The latter includes the following finding: "Many nonprofits are considering a fundamental change in organizational structure because of economic pressures such as. . . a shrinking supply of experienced leaders willing to remain in the sector for inadequate wages."

[2]Frederick Hertzberg, "One More Time: How Do You Motivate Employees?," *Harvard Business Review,* Vol. 65, No. 5, September–October 1987.

[3]Michael Beer, "The Transformation of the Human Resource Function: Resolving the Tension Between a Traditional Administrative and a New Strategic Role," *Human Resource Management,* Vol. 36, No. 1, Spring 1997.

[4]Independent Sector, "Leadership for the Common Good, Report on the Task Force on Future Leadership" (Washington, D.C.: Independent Sector).

[5]"The HP Way," 1989 company publication.

[6]Despite these impressive gains, GBRS still faced difficult challenges. After one of its key clients suffered a business setback that led it to drop its contract with GBRS, the nonprofit was forced to reorganize under Chapter 11. The reorganization has been successful, and GBRS is now focused on diversifying its contracts as additional protection in a volatile marketplace.

[7]Nora Lester, Melissa Lamson, and Neil Wollman, "How Staff Get Burned (Out) by Social Change Work," *Journal of Community Advocacy and Activism,* Vol. 2, June 1997, p. 88.

[8]Michael O'Neill, *The Third America: The Emergence of the Nonprofit Sector in the United States* (San Francisco: Jossey-Bass, 1989).

PART III

Mobilizing Stakeholders for High Performance

CHAPTER SEVEN

The Nonprofit Board: Creating a Culture of Performance

FRAMING QUESTIONS

▶ How can nonprofit boards support organizational capacity building?

▶ How can boards measure performance?

▶ How can group dynamics be managed to support a performance agenda?

The nonprofit board of directors operates at the intersection of public trust and organizational performance. It is up to the board, working with staff, to define the organization's mission, to develop a strategy for delivering on it, and to hold the organization accountable for getting results. No one underestimates the difficulty of this challenge. It has inspired both a large prescriptive literature and a growing corps of consultants who offer training and coaching. Many boards have used these resources to revise their structure and processes. They have reassessed how large they should be, how many committees they should have, how long members should serve, and how plans should be established. Rare is the board that does not have a clear mission statement, a strategic plan, and board processes in place. But all of these beg the question of how to move the organization from articulating a social *mission* to creating social *impact*, which is ultimately what the board should be accountable for. To bridge that gap requires organizational performance.

> *A board's job is not done until it has led its organization—not just to a clearer sense of its mission—but to better performance.*

Our cross-sector inquiry, drawing on board members from both sectors as well as consultants to boards, highlights both the potential and difficulty nonprofit boards face in creating the culture and capacity needed for high performance. Effective governance is not only more *important* for nonprofits than it is for for-profits, but also more *difficult* to achieve. On the one hand, nonprofit boards are more vital in ensuring performance and accountability because their organizations often function outside the market, which deprives them of critical feedback and accountability pressures. On the other hand, their job is also more difficult, for a number of reasons. For many nonprofits, performance is difficult to define, much less support and measure; the volunteer nature of nonprofit boards makes group dynamics even more complicated; and the added duties of fundraising saddle board members with distractions and conflicts, even as they keep the organization alive.

Does this mean the prospects for more effective board governance and, in turn, high-performing nonprofits are bleak? No. Luckily, nonprofit boards are not easily daunted by large challenges. They have an unparalleled resource in the form of committed leaders, who have already taken on the challenge of addressing important social issues they believe in. And, if they can reframe the board's mission based on a new understanding of how organizational performance contributes to impact, they are all the more likely to see their challenge as a meaningful one worth rising to. To succeed they need to revisit many of the basic aspects of governance, but with a view toward managing them for the special challenge of creating high performance organizations.

THE CHALLENGE FOR PERFORMANCE-ORIENTED BOARDS: GOVERNING UPSTREAM

Compared to their for-profit counterparts, nonprofit boards carry a much bigger burden in demanding and supporting performance. The for-profit board is one among several forces that are all aligned to support strong performance. To begin with, for-profit managers typically understand that building and sustaining organizational capacity is their raison d'être. No one has to convince them of the value of management and organizational capacity. And both boards and management can use market feedback to assess how well they are performing: customers, investors, and creditors all make evaluations that eventually show up in the bottom line. It's the board's job to assess that feedback and provide leadership in responding to it. If sales are down, the board needs to ask why, encourage or insist upon the development of improvement strategies, and use a blend of pressure and support to ensure that the CEO and staff get better results.

In contrast, the nonprofit board must often substitute for many of the feedback systems available in the marketplace. Nonprofit clients very often do not have a choice of providers, and are therefore unlikely to signal dissatisfaction by "voting with their feet." Foundations and government agencies that contract with nonprofits do not always have the same stake in improving organizational performance as, for example, investors do in a business. The funders of nonprofits can signal dissatisfaction by withdrawing support, but are much less likely to play the affirmative role of shareholder activist or institutional investor. Often when they do withdraw support, it is not because of the organization's failure to perform well, but instead because of a change in the foundation's program priorities or strategies.

Compounding the lack of market signals is the nonprofit environment described throughout this book: It generally undervalues organizational capacity. Donors are reluctant to pay for it, staff may be less interested in building it, and both may view it as a drain on program resources. Behind these attitudes is often a service culture that tends to view compassion and performance as wholly unrelated, if not mutually exclusive, assets. As a result, the nonprofit board carries a big burden. It is one of the only forces positioned to help a nonprofit develop the capacity it needs to deliver on its mission. But to play that role, it has to become a change agent willing to challenge nonprofit conventions about the value of organizational capacity.

> *Like the staff that manage upstream against these forces, boards willing to play this role will have to govern upstream.*

THE FIRST STEP: DEFINING AND MEASURING PERFORMANCE

Building organizational capacity and a culture that will sustain it starts with understanding the real role and value of organizational performance. Most boards approach performance and performance measurement as a matter of strategic planning and financial management. As vital as both functions are, they are not enough. A strategic plan outlining where the organization wants to go is worth little unless the organization has the capacity to get there, and the resources to create the impact the plan seeks. Strategic plans rarely take into account the adaptive capacities that an organization will need to deliver on its mission. For example, they might envision innovation, but provide no guidance on how to support it. Or they might stress the importance of high quality staff, but not address the resources needed to attract and retain them. Or they might elevate "quality service" as a central value, but with no reference to the tools and resources needed to achieve and sustain quality. Similarly, good financial practices, though critical for sustaining the organization, do not directly address the challenge of creating social impact.

134

Instead of demanding and measuring the adaptive capacities that do drive performance, many boards end up focusing almost exclusively on financial performance for several reasons. First, it is important. Organizations cannot survive, much less become effective or efficient, unless their finances are well managed. Second, assessing financial performance falls clearly into the "oversight" and fiduciary responsibility role; it does not raise questions of board meddling in management. Third, for board members with business experience, focusing on the numbers is a natural. They are competent, comfortable, and can take satisfaction in their value-added, especially in cases where the organization's managers have strong programmatic expertise but weak administrative skills. And financial oversight generates familiar, tangible tasks for board members, who can work on audit, finance, and fundraising.

Although we tend to consider financial management a complex, technical practice, the information it provides is in some ways very crude and has little bearing on improving the organization's capacity for performance.

> *Knowing whether and by how much an organization is in the red or the black does not speak at all to what the organization is doing well, or whether and how it should be improved.*

Financial data is also backward looking. It speaks to past performance, not to future performance. Even setting future goals (e.g., for growth in revenue) is no assurance that an organization is creating social impact.

In addition to developing a vision and providing fiscal oversight, boards have an opportunity, and an obligation, to build the organization's adaptive capacity, a process that begins with defining and measuring performance. Boards need to ask themselves what kind of information they and the staff need in order to succeed, and then ensure that the staff has the support to gather and use it. We saw in benchmarking how the board of the Boston Ballet took a lead role in studying best practices in developing a positive public image, a priority the board had set. The board of Wellspring House, Inc. took the lead in organizing a planning process that ensured that the voices of many community stakeholders, including homeless families, were incorporated into their work. Developing information, performance targets, and metrics on issues like these, which address more than financial performance, is fundamental to advancing the work of a performance-oriented board. The nonprofit board is a critical force in supporting and demanding this type of capacity.

Performance measurement along these other dimensions is vital to effective governance. E.B. Wilson, chairman of Executive Service Corps of New England and a member of both corporate and nonprofit boards, notes a "convergence of good practices" among both nonprofit and for-profit boards. He sees at the center of good practice the conversion of "strategic plans into goals and objectives for the chief executive officer and for the board." The motivation of individual board members, moreover, turns on measuring their progress in meeting these goals: "If you're going to drive board performance and drive individual ownership of their role on the board, you must relate them to goals." Boards can measure their performance against financial goals without ever considering measures for other dimensions of performance, like quality, innovation, or staff motivation.

RECONCILING HIGH PERFORMANCE AND THE GROUP DYNAMICS OF VOLUNTEERS

No matter what function they are playing, boards are complicated by the very nature of group dynamics. These challenges, combined with the nature of some volunteer nonprofit boards, are only greater for boards that are serious about improving organizational performance. Translating "group leadership" into results is inherently complicated. For example, when a group is responsible for outcomes, how can members develop a sense of personal accountability? How can some, with special expertise or assignments, be prevented from dominating others? How does the group manage the rivalries, impatience, resentments? Brooke Mahoney, president of Volunteer Consulting Group, a New York nonprofit that supports nonprofit board development, says the problem is that "We take people who are *hierarchically* trained and we put them into a group process where there are no clear roles. And it's very, very difficult. Sitting groups of trustees will tolerate behavior they would never tolerate in a hierarchical structure."

Few people are trained to handle the challenge. "We are pitiful as a culture," says Mahoney, "at helping men and women understand the skills of civic leadership and what is involved in being a player in our democracy." Nonprofit boards, in fact, often end up recruiting people who are essential, but ill equipped for the challenges of group processes. On the one hand, their social mission may compel organizations to involve disempowered residents, who by definition have limited education, formal leadership experience, or board experience. On the other hand, the need for expertise and/or clout also leads nonprofits to seek out talented business leaders. As Barbara Taylor, Richard Chait, and Thomas Holland have observed, however, the problem is that they have often succeeded and been rewarded for their decisiveness, independence, and strong wills, not for their ability to build consensus and work collaboratively.[1]

For the many nonprofits that have committed to create a more inclusive board, diversity itself may complicate group dynamics, even as it enriches the collective experience and perspective of the board. Board members on diverse boards need to switch from a hierarchy to team framework, while at the same time encountering new cultural or social norms as the profile of board members changes. It can be harder for the group to work as a team when there is no single social code to guide interactions.

These challenges are only magnified when a volunteer nonprofit board tries to develop a culture of performance. Board members are driven by a commitment to a social vision and an altruistic desire to make a contribution to their community or society. Yet there appears to be something in the nature of these volunteer boards that makes effective governance what Taylor and colleagues call "a rare and unnatural act." For instance, many have observed that business leaders, often sought by nonprofit boards in hopes of improving the performance of their organizations, seem to lose their businesslike performance focus when entering the nonprofit board room.[3] Why does it seem difficult for boards to reconcile their social commitment with their responsibility to contribute to effective organizational performance?

The first obstacle for many volunteer nonprofit board members may be time. Several of our observers pointed out that changing work patterns may be thinning the ranks of the traditional board members. As businesses become more competitive, what was once the norm, that CEOs and senior corporate managers would be visibly active in civic and social affairs, may now be more the exception. Workplace pressure is only compounded in families with two working parents. And it has always been difficult for poor residents of distressed communities, raising families with few supports, to find time for civic affairs. These time pressures undoubtedly influence the willingness of people to serve on boards. And once they are serving on boards, how willing will they be to create more work and pressure by taking on a complex agenda of organizational performance?

A second obstacle, perhaps even more important than the time available to board members, is the expectations board members bring to their work. Most people serve to do good, and to feel good by doing good. They want to connect with the socially relevant issues their day jobs may not deal with.

> *Dealing with organizational performance, particularly if it involves conflicts, can frustrate the desire to feel good by serving on a board.*

One board member conceded that a board meeting is often like a "social gathering where you almost don't want to ask a hard question." The problem is that assessing and developing strategies for effective performance often requires tension. As E.B. Wilson of Executive Service Corps expressed it, "good board performance involves an active, engaged, collegial tension between the board and operating management. If you don't have that, you have to insist on it as a board."

A third obstacle is the interest of board members. Many board members are concerned mostly with the organization's social mission. They simply may not want to tackle what may seem like ancillary, organizational issues. And the management of nonprofits, not wanting boards to meddle in operational matters, are unlikely to create a mandate for a board-led organizational performance agenda. Some board members, moreover, will have no organizational or management experience to bring to the challenge. Finally, Brooke Mahoney has encountered yet another scenario, where efforts to bring management and organizational depth to the board are met with outright hostility. Writing about one such clash, when a bank executive joined the board of a dance company, she summed up the dynamics by subtitling her piece "Do bankers eat artists for breakfast?"

It is tempting to conclude that the solution to the problems of volunteer boards is to compensate board members. One of our observers, who serves on paid for-profit boards and unpaid nonprofit boards, feels a "contractual relationship" with the organization that pays him but also feels close to the nonprofits that don't "because I believe in what they're doing for the community." Another remarked that "I'm feeling closer now to the boards where I don't get paid because of the crises we've gone through. I feel committed to keep the board committed."

In the end, compensation may induce more people to serve in the first place, or to attend to board business more diligently, but the real question is: What will change the culture of boards so that they demand and support performance? After all, nonprofit staff are compensated, and they often exhibit many of the same deficits, indifference to or suspicion about organizational performance issues as unpaid board members. It is the nature of the work, more than the commitment to it, that needs to be considered in new ways.

Despite the problems posed by group dynamics and the nature of a volunteer board, nonprofits have at least two distinctive assets to bring to bear. First, there is probably more training, technical assistance, and "how to" advice for nonprofit board members than there is for for-profit board members. Though this may reflect a greater need for such help in the nonprofit sector, where the challenges of governing are so complex, it means that resources are available to many boards to help not only with group-process challenges, but many other aspects of board performance as well. Second, much of the nonprofit sector is actively committed to principles of empowerment and participation. In this environment, the readiness and willingness of board members to rethink their collaboration may be an advantage. Both training and a philosophical commitment to participation should be harnessed to tackle the problems of group leadership.

Boards, like staff, need well defined challenges and expectations for performance. The rewards of meeting those challenges will likely motivate members to tolerate the conflicts and complexity that come with improving organizational performance. Board members can take steps to ensure that they do not become exclusively focused on performance at the cost of personal satisfaction in the accomplishments of the nonprofit. For example, it could be useful to arrange special events, outside the board's regular work schedule, where members can celebrate and take satisfaction in the work of the nonprofit, and in their contributions to it, while board meetings are reserved for business. The use of small, ad hoc groups can resolve some of the efficiency and conflict aversion problems of larger groups. Within the board room, it will be important to help board members focus on setting and reaching goals. As we saw in our cases on human resources, nothing motivates people as effectively as the opportunity to take on significant work that allows them to see the results of their efforts.

FUNDRAISING: A DISTRACTION OR A RESOURCE FOR PERFORMANCE?

Most nonprofits depend on board members to donate or raise funds for the organization. While an organization that has a board willing to raise funds is not well advised to give it up, it is worth considering how this added duty (which for-profit board members do not assume) affects the board's performance agenda. First, raising funds consumes an enormous amount of time. And as with nonprofit executives, who often spend up to half their time on fundraising, board time spent on fundraising, whether discussing it as a group or working on it individually, is time *not* spent on something else. Second, and more subtly, engaging the board in raising funds influences the way they think about performance. Fundraising goals can be clear and compelling, and therefore very useful in mobilizing board members. But if they crowd out other performance goals, fundraising targets can be dangerous. Increasing revenues or donations does not necessarily increase the quality of services or the capacity of the organization to deliver. It is tempting to substitute growth in revenues for mission fulfillment.

Recruiting wealthy board members or foundation leaders, while obviously a savvy move, has its downside if it displaces members with important perspectives and expertise. Another hazardous consequence is that staff will begin deferring, perhaps even unconsciously, to these wealthy (or otherwise powerful) board members. A board that is clearly focused on a performance agenda, however, can contain this risk: pet projects or preferences will have to be measured against a clear strategy and set of organizational priorities. If the board can limit the potential for undue influence, funders can make important contributions sharing the benefits of their work with a wide variety of organizations.

If they cannot afford to give up their fundraising role, what can boards do to ensure that fundraising supports their capacity-building efforts? Perhaps most significantly, they can challenge the norms and attitudes of donors about the value of organizational support. For example, they can challenge the impulse that led philanthropist Ted Turner, upon making a one-billion-dollar commitment to United Nations causes, to vow that none of his funds would support overhead.

> *Board members can help funders distinguish between unproductive overhead and real value-creating organizational capacity.*

They can request funding for general operating support or for special performance-improving programs (like benchmarking or quality systems) and for fundraising itself, to assess, for example, whether revenue-generating strategies are viable for the organization. By raising money for the organization's efforts to improve its effectiveness, board members can make the exhausting job of fundraising serve an organization-improvement agenda.

CONCLUSION

To succeed in building organizational capacity as a resource for the social missions they believe in, boards need to build a *culture* that values organizational performance. At the outset, asking the right questions will be more important than having the precise answers, processes, or strategies for improving performance. A sustainable commitment to organizational performance needs to start with questions the board really cares about: What difference are we making in the lives of our community? Where could we do better? And as they probe these questions, boards will be better positioned to set goals and investigate options for meeting them. As they define, demand, support, and measure performance, they can leave to staff the work of implementing new organizational processes. In many cases, staff will welcome the board's attention to their organizational needs. And as capacity building leads to better performance, the clients and communities served by the nonprofit will reap the ultimate benefits of organizational performance—greater social impact. Then boards can take real satisfaction in doing good by governing well.

ADDITIONAL READING

Bowen, William G., *Inside the Boardroom: Governance by Directors and Trustees*. New York: John Wiley & Sons, 1994.

Chait, Richard P., Thomas P. Holland, and Barbara E. Taylor. *Improving the Performance of Governing Boards*. Phoenix: Oryx Press, 1996.

Drucker, Peter. "Lessons for Successful Nonprofit Governance," *Nonprofit Management & Leadership*, Vol. 1, No. 1, Fall 1990, pp. 7–13.

Duca, Diane. *Nonprofit Boards: Roles, Responsibilities and Performance*. New York: John Wiley & Sons, 1996.

Hall, Peter Dobkin. *Inventing the Nonprofit Sector and Other Essays on Philanthropy, Voluntarism, and Nonprofit Organizations*. Baltimore: Johns Hopkins University Press, 1992.

Matthiasen III, Karl. *Board Passages: Three Key Stages in a Nonprofit Board's Life Cycle*. Washington, DC: Center for Nonprofit Boards, 1990.

Salmon, Walter J. "Crisis Prevention: How to Gear Up Your Board," *Harvard Business Review*, January–February 1993, pp. 68–75.

Taylor, Barbara E., Richard P. Chait, and Thomas P. Holland. "The New Work of the Nonprofit Board," *Harvard Business Review*, September–October, 1996.

Wood, Miriam, ed. *Nonprofit Boards and Leadership: Cases on Governance, Change, and Board-Staff Dynamics*. San Francisco: Jossey-Bass, 1996.

Zander, Alvin. *Making Boards Effective: The Dynamics of Nonprofit Governance*. San Francisco: Jossey-Bass, 1993.

ENDNOTES

[1]Barbara E. Taylor, Richard P. Chait, and Thomas P. Holland, "The New Work of the Nonprofit Board." (*Harvard Business Review*, September–October, 1996.)

[2]William G. Bowen, "When a Business Leader Joins a Nonprofit Board." (*Harvard Business Review*, September–October, 1994, pp. 38–44.)

CHAPTER EIGHT

The National Office: Leading Program Expansion by Supporting High Performance

FRAMING QUESTIONS

▶ How does a national office measure and manage local performance?

▶ How does the role of a nonprofit change when it moves from local operator to a national office for multiple sites?

▶ What services does a national office provide to support local performance?

Program expansion (as we discuss in the Introduction and Part I) is a critical challenge for the nonprofit sector. Hoping to benefit more people and communities, many who have developed successful programs look for ways to expand them to new sites. In turning their attention to expansion, many program operators find themselves in new territory, where the challenges are not only difficult but ill-defined. The national organizations profiled in this chapter have contended with all aspects of managing organizational growth or program expansion. They grant that the early stages of expansion—identifying new sites, cultivating local supporters and funders, or finding good local operators—are complicated in their own right. Ultimately, though, the national organizations view these challenges of getting to large scale-operation as only the beginning. As they took on the role of national organizations supporting local affiliates, they began fulfilling a range of new functions. Among the most critical are those that help affiliates perform effectively.

To a large extent, the national offices that support local affiliates become agents for promoting and supporting high performance. Particularly for nonprofits, few other stakeholders are positioned to become champions for high performance. Among the many functions they fill, this is perhaps the most challenging, and the most valuable. All of the national organizations profiled here—nonprofits, for-profits, franchisors, company-owned, and associations—defined their mission and function in remarkably similar terms. In many crucial ways, they are capacity-builders as much as they are program expanders. Specifically, the cases suggest three themes that underlie the challenge of succeeding as a national organization:

1. In moving from program (or retail) operator to national office, they transform the function, objectives, strategies, and culture of their organizations—all of which require radical commitment to a growth agenda.
2. In addition to clear commitment to this new mission, program expanders develop new capacities for learning and communicating about the essential elements of successful program operation—starting with a proving period when they refine the program and on through to their sustaining role, when they become a resource for continuous learning at the local level.
3. As they shift from serving clients to serving the local affiliates who serve those clients, the national offices also play a critical role in driving local performance—both by defining performance standards and holding affiliates accountable for meet-

ing them. Because it inevitably creates tensions between the local and central operators, this role creates its own challenges for the program expander.

This work is very different from the work of program operation. The cases presented here raise new ideas about how nonprofits can think about and tackle the challenge of program expansion.

BRUEGGER'S BAGELS

Bruegger's Bagels was founded in 1983 in Troy, New York by Nordahl Brue, an attorney, and Michael Dresser, a commercial builder. By 1996, it had expanded to 450 locations in 31 states. About two-thirds of these shops are "affiliated franchises" in which Dresser and Brue are partners with the local franchise operator. Sales for 1997 were $210 million, and Bruegger's was designated by leading business journals variously as one of the "Top 50 Growth Chains," "The Nation's Best Franchises," and the "Marketing 100."

> *From the outset, Bruegger's founders were dedicated not to running a bagel shop but to building a bagel franchise system, and they understood the radical difference between the two.*

"Franchising is a different business activity from running restaurants," Brue emphasized, "with a totally different mindset, a different set of customers, and the franchisor must have a different orientation and approach."

That "orientation and approach" aimed at creating a service that would succeed at large scale over time. Their first step was to develop and test a product and service concept that would appeal to franchise operators and to customers nationwide. "The reason people buy franchises is because they see that the prototype works," Brue explained. To deliver that assurance, Bruegger's adopted what

Brue calls "a six-by-six-by-six strategy." It decided to test six stores in each of six regions over six years to find the winning formula. "Our notion was that we had to have 36 units operating in a variety of different markets in a variety of different locations" in order to prove that Bruegger's would work.

Bruegger's operated these first stores in partnership with local operators, using the stores as laboratories to test and refine its products and service approaches. "Our decision to involve local partners was critical," says Brue. "It's important to have someone with a real stake out in the field." By the end of the trial period, Bruegger's had found the right balance among what Brue calls the "three P's: people, product, and place—or the service, food, and ambiance." And franchisees bought into the formula, propelling Bruegger's rapid growth.

As a franchisor, Bruegger's strategy was to focus on the success of each operating unit. Bruegger's concluded that, to succeed, each one must pass a series of tests, or "the five unit elements": unit economics, management, operation, marketing, and location. On location, for example, "a hundred yards in a metropolitan area can mean the difference literally between success and failure." On management, "you change your manager and within 30 days the sales are up over 20 percent. You've got a leader who makes an impact on every one of the people serving the counter. The line speed is up. The customers notice it. All of a sudden things are working."

The role of the franchisor is to support those local capacities by developing new capacities for learning, quality improvement, and product development at headquarters. Specifically, Brue described five "system" functions that the franchisor handles to support performance at the local level:

1. Understanding the customer, especially emerging consumer trends that local operators may have trouble assessing.

2. Definition of the product and service concepts, guided by the KISS ("keep it simple, stupid") principle, which states that the simpler the design of the unit operation, the fewer the elements that require discretion, and the more predictable and replicable the service.

3. Information exchange to share best practices and find out what doesn't work and get rid of it.

4. Protection of the brand through enforcement of quality standards.

5. System economics—sufficient units to achieve market penetration and "regional" performance.

It became Bruegger's job to develop management and organizational capacities to support these functions, none of which can be handled as well at the local level.

SUMMERBRIDGE NATIONAL

Summerbridge National supports the operation of Summerbridge programs, which offer summer study, tutorials, and mentoring to academically talented but underserved middle school students. The program's objective is to prepare these students for academically rigorous college preparatory high schools. High school and college students provide the teaching, mentoring, and counseling to the Summerbridge students. The national operation provides technical assistance and support to schools operating the program, including curriculum materials, operations manuals, matching grants, conferences and forums, national recognition, and research and evaluation. In 1996, there were 33 programs operating in 28 cities across the United States (and through a sister program in Hong Kong).

Unlike Bruegger's founders, Lois Loofbourrow, the founder of Summerbridge, initially was not interested in expanding the program. Launched at the private University High School in San Francisco in 1978, Summerbridge remained a single-site operation for the next 11 years. Although Summerbridge's operators had no growth ambitions, they were eager to share their ideas and experiences with the many visitors who were intrigued by the program. Loofbourrow calls these " 'the barnyard years.' We had a lot of seeds that we left around with the gate open. Anyone could come in and pick up any crumbs that were useful and do anything they wanted with them. . . . That was very exciting. And out of those years came a whole group of people who came and observed, took what they wanted, and left the rest—and lots of programs started."

Persuaded, Loofbourrow launched Summerbridge National in 1991 to help other high schools implement the program and to support some programs started without Summerbridge's involvement during the "barnyard years." Since Summerbridge National would not have "line authority" over these affiliates, it instead looked to identify and share the core elements that made Summerbridge successful. These became the basis for a memorandum of understanding between the national office and affiliates. The agreement laid out both broad goals and principles, as well as nonnegotiable requirements, including:

- Focus on a single core objective—creating programs that are "academically rigorous and empower students with the necessary skills to succeed eventually in college preparatory programs."
- Programs could not depart, in the first year of operation, from the model without approval from National.
- Required collaboration among the programs, including local financing for travel to other sites and an emphasis on accommodating visitors and observers.
- At least two visits in the first year by Summerbridge National staff.

Some requirements were defined or amended in response to an early, fundamental program decision that the National board faced. A prospective program operator in Cambridge, MA proposed a major variation on the model: She wanted to operate the program not in a private high school but in the local public high school. This proposed deviation from the original program forced Summerbridge National to become more specific about which features of the program were essential and which were alterable.

As she began assessing which features produced success, what standards operators would have to meet, and how to facilitate operators' communications and learning, Loofbourrow was defining the new role of the national office. She was no longer in the business of directly serving youth, but of helping affiliates develop the capacity for effective direct service.

MACTEMPS, INC.

MacTemps, Inc. is a temporary staffing company started in Cambridge, Massachusetts and incorporated in 1986. MacTemps is currently in 28 cities in nine countries, with 220 employees and 7,000 temporary workers. Sales in 1997 were $107 million. Founded by three Harvard College juniors—John Chuang, Steven Kapner, and Mia Wenjen, with a $5,000 loan cosigned by their parents—MacTemps started as a self-serve desktop publishing center where students could use high-end desktop publishing equipment to design and print documents. It later evolved into a temporary staffing company offering a range of services: software specialists; creative designers (such as graphic design, art direction, photography, and copy writing); and, most recently, a service that provides computer network contractors.

Growth was a key goal for MacTemps. After opening several of the self-serve stores in the Cambridge area, catering mostly to students, Chuang and his partners discovered that the economics of the business would not support growth. As Jae-Ho Synn, vice president of MacTemps, explained at our roundtable, they began looking for a different business concept, one that was "scalable." Recalling that they had occasionally received calls asking if they had temps they could send out, the founders decided to place an ad in a computer publication to see if high-skilled desktop-publisher temps might be a viable service. Their pitch was simple: "You didn't just buy any computer, don't hire just any temp to use it."[1] They discovered the demand for Mac specialist temps was enormous.

Although MacTemps was eager to grow, it had few formal plans or systems to manage the growth process. "We made a lot of mistakes," says Synn "and I guess it's safe to say that we were trying to figure things out as we went along." Though weak on formal systems and strategies, MacTemps was strong on some fundamentals:

clarity about its service concept; a strong company culture; and a simple, "first mover advantage" strategy to capture important markets early.

The very name "MacTemps" has helped the company maintain a clear focus. Synn admits that even though the name is a misnomer now (they don't only work on Macs, and they do permanent placements as well as temps), MacTemps has always been something that people could understand and has remained very meaningful for the development of the organization.

A strong culture of trust and cohesion also helped the company grow, despite the lack of formal systems. The development of the MacTemps system, according to Synn, was driven by a "decision-making process loosely defined by a commitment to certain common principles." The trust and common commitment of this network was particularly important early on, when billing was still handled by phone and the company did not own a fax machine. Formal, continuous oversight was difficult in these conditions.

After detecting signs of "internally generated stress," says Synn, "we standardized a lot of things." New systems were created to address a number of challenges—turnover, customer satisfaction, and losing niche to other staffing companies. "We've instituted some systems for customer service. We have a 110 percent guarantee. We have a very robust testing and training program." In this case, weakening unit performance and other negative indicators provided the wakeup call to the central unit that the system needed more capacity, particularly to support the learning, quality assurance, and training that affiliates would be hard pressed to undertake on their own. In spite of these changes, culture remains primary at MacTemps, and people still come before systems. Synn admits that, "It's horribly inefficient at times but it can work."

YOUTHBUILD USA

YouthBuild USA is a national intermediary and support center for YouthBuild programs, over 100 of which have been established in 34 states, serving over 4,600 young adults annually. YouthBuild programs help young people ages 16 to 24 acquire construction skills, complete a high school education, and receive leadership training while rehabilitating or constructing new housing for low-income and homeless people in their communities. Participants spend alternate weeks on the job site and in school. Along with skill development, the program also promotes involvement in a positive peer group and in the community.

YouthBuild USA provides a range of services—consultation, conferences, publications, and research—to program operators through two vehicles. Under a grant from the federal Department of Housing and Urban Development, YouthBuild USA is the major technical assistance provider for program operators who are funded by HUD, to whom Congress appropriated a total of $192 million for YouthBuild programs between 1993 and 1997. Through the YouthBuild USA Affiliated Network, the organization serves a smaller set of program operators—those who have voluntarily committed to create and enforce joint standards governing the design and implementation of the program. (As we will discuss later, the Affiliated Network was created by program operators who feared that newer, federally funded program operators would not necessarily value the original model and, by interpreting it liberally, might damage the reputation of the "brand.")

In 1978, Dorothy Stoneman founded the Youth Action Program, YouthBuild's predecessor, in East Harlem. Its goal was to engage young people in the design and implementation of community improvement projects, one of which was rehabilitation of housing. In 1984 they launched a citywide replication process after securing city funding for nine programs. But the absence of technical assistance and a clearly communicated program prototype caused five of them to fail within a short time. To correct that problem, in 1988 the successful New York City operators collaborated with Stoneman in writing a program manual, and launching YouthBuild USA to provide guidance to future programs.

Initially, YouthBuild focused on promoting the program concept to anyone who wanted to use it to improve communities. "We wanted to share ideas, not own them; spread inspiration and information, not profit from them. . . . We thought YouthBuild could become a generic and widespread concept, like daycare centers, or youth corps. We gave the name away freely."

> *But when YouthBuild achieved an important part of what it wanted, significant federal funding to support program operators nationwide, it began to rethink the tradeoffs between* widespread *and* disciplined *implementation of the model.*

When HUD made it clear that it would not force organizations to use the YouthBuild model literally, YouthBuild began to distinguish its two roles as growth agent—one for those who were inspired by the concept but would implement it largely as they wanted; and another for a community of program operators who believed that the real value of the program was in its comprehensive design and philosophical commitment to leadership and community development, and who therefore supported a clear program model and consistent implementation guidelines.

True to YouthBuild's grassroots culture, it was the members who urged on the national entity the role of developing and enforcing standards. As the first generation of about 15 YouthBuild operations considered the care and work that had gone into growing and sustaining their operations, they worried that newcomers without similar commitment would diminish the value of the YouthBuild name and reputation. Neither Stoneman nor the program operators viewed the model as immutable. As a group, they determined which elements of the program were essential if an operation was to use the name, and compliance with these guidelines is now a condition for using the YouthBuild name.

YouthBuild USA also provides the local operator with benchmarks for gauging their performance (another capacity that affiliates would be hard pressed to develop on their own). The national office has learned that a successful unit should retain 70 percent of participants for the full length of the program, and see 95 percent of those completing it get placed in jobs with average wages of $7.00 per hour.

MAKING THE COMMITMENT TO THE NEW ROLE OF A NATIONAL OFFICE

The organizations profiled here all understood that successful expansion requires a radical, fundamental commitment. Expansion shapes (or reshapes) every aspect of the organization—mission, goals, strategies, and culture—and cannot be successful without a clear understanding of and commitment to the new role. Bruegger's never thought of anything but expansion. At the outset, the company founders wanted a successful franchise system, not a successful bagel shop that might or might not later choose to expand. At MacTemps, the decision to find a "scalable" business came early on. It led the founders first to develop a new service concept that would better support growth. Eventually, Synn explained, MacTemps' commitment to growth hardened to the point where "It was not a choice not to grow." Both YouthBuild and Summerbridge made similar, radical commitments to expansion. They ended up creating new organizations, launched specifically to manage program expansion.

All four organizations understood that the difference between operating a program at one site and aiming to expand it to many is profound. With that decision, the very mission of the organization changes, from offering a service to a local community to helping other program operators offer that service to their own communities.

> *The organization managing expansion is not doing more of something, but doing something different.*

(The sectors may differ on the timing of their intention to expand. Many for-profits are launched with ambitions for large-scale expansion; whereas nonprofits often start life as a single-site operator that only later makes the commitment to expansion.) And if the organization's board and staff are not clearly committed to and equipped for this new mission, their challenge will be all the more complicated.

Clarity and strength of commitment are all the more important for nonprofits, because growth is often a contested goal. As one management consultant working with both for-profits and nonprofits expressed it, for business people the decision to grow is natural—"like breathing"—but for nonprofits, it typically "creates a lot of internal strife." Consistent with that observation, a nonprofit founder recounted in one of our roundtables: "As we started to grow, I could see a divide in my staff. There were the people who said, 'Keep growing; I'm here because this is a cutting-edge new organization and I want to see it be huge and national.' At the same time I had staff who were saying 'Why grow? It just means more work.'"

The conflicts may have several causes. Some nonprofit employees and trustees may be dedicated to improving their own community. They understand that managing expansion will launch them into an entirely new role, and decide it is not one that interests them. Others may object more to what they perceive as a growth culture and values. Roland Hodson, an international development specialist, argues that many nonprofit employees share a common "suspicion of hierarchical frameworks," which they associate with growing organizations. In organizations that have grown significantly, many indulge in a "romantic harking back to the way things were when the organization was smaller."[2] They may fear the organization will become too "bureaucratic," or that it will compromise values. Nonprofits cannot presume that all their stakeholders will support expansion. They have to build support for it.

In weighing expansion options, it would help to understand not only that effective expansion requires a new commitment but also that it requires new capacities on the part of the national office. What is the new business of expansion about? What are the implications for an organization's culture and values? What is the new work? Our cases suggest that the national office dedicates itself to supporting high performance among program operators, primarily by assuming learning and quality control functions.

DEVELOPING LEARNING SYSTEMS THAT SUPPORT HIGH PERFORMANCE

The organizations profiled played two learning roles, both vital to successful expansion. First, they used a proving period to develop and refine their services. They not only asked whether an organization worked, but probed how it worked and what processes supported effective outcomes. They then converted these lessons into clear operating practices and principles that others could use. Second, once expansion was under way, they supported learning among local managers, to help them sustain or improve their performance. In all of our cases, their strength was not only in their program or service design, but in their capacity to develop new organizational processes both for learning and for teaching organizations how to operate the program successfully.

The Proving Period: A Foundation for Expansion

A proving period enables an organization to prepare for expansion by (1) testing the service to ensure it is worth growing in the first place and that it demonstrates value to those who will manage the local operation; (2) improving the service based on early feedback; and (3) understanding which organizational processes enable successful delivery of the service, so that other program operators can be trained and supported. The organizations in our roundtable all responded to the need for a proving period differently, raising two key questions: How deliberate does a proving process have to be? (In other words, do the founders need to know from the outset that they are in a proving period that will lead to expansion?) And what exactly are they trying to prove during this time—whether the program works, what makes it work, or both?

Our organizations demonstrated different levels of intent and sophistication during their proving periods. Bruegger's proving period, like its growth ambitions, was highly developed. The six-by-six-by-six strategy allowed them to study and improve on different combinations of "people, place, and product." Bruegger's set out to understand what mix would be most effective, and therefore most likely to attract franchisees. At the other end of the spectrum is MacTemps, which felt it had to grow quickly in order to seize the "first-mover advantage." Initially, they knew that there was a demand for their services, but not at first about how their services should be managed to meet that demand in more markets over time. Their fast ramp-up and informal approach made analysis of these service-delivery variables impossible. It was only later, as client demands and software became more complex, that they backed into the proving process. They began offering training and support programs to assess workers' skills in a more systematic way.

In between these precisely engineered and highly entrepreneurial demonstration periods are YouthBuild and Summerbridge. These demonstrations are most striking for their length. Summerbridge was at one site for 11 years before expanding. YouthBuild first operated one program in East Harlem for six years, then operated additional programs elsewhere in New York City for another four years, and then launched its national expansion. While nonprofits often tend to define a proving period by conventional grant cycles (e.g., in terms of a three-year pilot-program grant), these two organizations moved much more slowly. While these preexpansion periods were long, were they really proving periods? That is, were the nonprofits deliberately collecting information about outcomes and processes that would support expansion later on? Yes and no.

Summerbridge, although it had no intention of expanding during its early years, was assessing and documenting its performance. When the time came to expand, Loofbourrow says Summerbridge was "funder ready." They had a clear program design and documented results. But since they had not been contemplating an active role in coaching or teaching others to operate the program, they had not focused on documenting the processes that created success. Indeed, they were operating at only one site, with no basis for figuring out which variables contribute to success. So when they faced their first decision about major program modification (whether Cambridge could run the program at a public high school), they had little information about process to guide them. It was hard for them to gauge what exactly had produced such consistent success at University High, and then to compare those process features to the situation at the Cambridge public school. As the program expanded into new environments, Summerbridge National was able to document variations in performance and consider what processes supported success. Like MacTemps, it was able to make midcourse corrections during the expansion.

YouthBuild's first cycle of expansion in New York City was an important proving period. Stoneman explained that the failures of the first city-funded programs, offered without technical assistance, eliminated their "optimistic trust that having money and a good idea would insure success." As with Summerbridge and MacTemps, the proving period was in large part retrospective. As the early program operators began writing the first handbook, they began reflecting on the performance of the most successful operators and attempted to capture their lessons for future replication. The proximity of the sites made it easier to assess the most common errors and the critical success factors.

The length of proving periods may be longer than nonprofits normally assume (six, nine, and 11 years for three of these organizations, versus the three years of a conventional nonprofit pilot). But even more important is the proving strategy: How is the organization testing and refining the program? Is it studying and documenting the organizational processes that support success? These questions are likely to be critical in equipping the organization to help other program operators understand their success.

Clarity: The Key to Learning

It is not enough to develop and refine a program during the proving period. Successful expansion requires that local program operators understand clearly which features are essential, and why and how they work. The national office needs to analyze and document this vital information as clearly and precisely as possible. All of the organizations at the roundtable struggled to achieve this clarity. Bruegger's six-year trial period was aimed at discovering and clarifying the right franchise concept. It not only articulated the product line but also the processes for delivering that product successfully. Both had to be clear to hundreds of managers across a large franchise system. MacTemps also emphasized clarity and simplicity, which were probably all the more important to an organization with very few formal systems. The service concept was articulated every time the name "MacTemps" was spoken.

With adequate analysis and documentation, even a complex program or service can become clear. YouthBuild USA has used its handbook, which has been revised eight times since it was first developed, to codify what is known about how individual Youth-Build organizations can be successful. Despite many attempts to change and enhance the model, Stoneman reports that, time and again, people come back in the end to say, "I can tell you from my own experience that it works when you follow the book," suggesting that YouthBuild has succeeded in clarifying the essential components for success.

Continuous Learning

In most cases, the role of the national office is not to offer onetime instruction in the operation of a program. Instead, the national office becomes an ongoing resource for learning and improvement. Several managers argued the real value of a national network is the accumulation of experience and knowledge that is gained by doing something over and over. Particularly among the nonprofits, where the relationship between central and unit operations is often voluntary, learning services are highly valued. Conferences, publications, newsletters, and site visits are all organized by the central organization to help affiliates gain new insights and practical techniques, and share best practices for improving program delivery.

These continuous learning services also enable members to connect with and support each other, which in turn supports their morale. Part of the appeal of nonprofit networks, Stoneman suggests, lies in their ability to empower nonprofit leaders:

People in the nonprofit sector are driven by their commitment, their vision, their cause, but plagued by the feeling of powerlessness. What you get from a network is a sense of greater power, greater efficacy, greater ability to have an impact on larger issues than you can do alone. And so as long as that network is not oppressive and overcontrolling or insulting, and you feel a kinship with the other members, it can bring much greater value into your life.

MEASURING, SUPPORTING, AND DEMANDING PERFORMANCE BY AFFILIATES

As national organizations explained their role and strategies, they emphasized repeatedly that their most important contribution was in supporting and sustaining successful performance at the local level. Without consistent high quality, even large-scale expansion is a hollow, and probably short-lived, achievement. National organizations use several approaches to sustain quality performance. They define performance standards, measure local performance against these standards, and use a combination of coaching and enforcement to ensure that affiliates meet those standards. In effect, the program expanders help hold affiliates accountable to their clients and to other operators who have a stake in the program's reputation. In addition to playing this quality-assurance and support role, the national office must manage the tensions that arise as a central authority seeks to monitor and influence affiliates.

The Value of Performance Standards

The national organizations in our inquiry stressed two dimensions of performance. First, it is a matter of mission. For businesses, quality is the key to customer satisfaction and profits; for nonprofits it leads to social impact. Second, national organizations focus on quality for the benefit of affiliates. Protecting the "brand" or reputation of the program becomes another service they deliver to their affiliates. Customers and prospective franchisors need to know that a franchise name stands for consistent quality, and nonprofit program operators all rely on the reputation of their program to build support in their community and among funders. It was individual

YouthBuild program operators, in fact, who insisted on clear program standards. They wanted to be sure the YouthBuild name stood for quality, and that their reputations would not be harmed by inept program execution by others in the system.

To serve both clients and operators, national organizations impose minimum requirements on their operators. Bruegger's, Summerbridge, and YouthBuild all established handbooks clearly outlining standards and procedures, not just as training tools but also as rules that must be adhered to as a condition of using the program. This is a far cry from "the barnyard" approach of sharing freely and letting a hundred flowers bloom. In shifting from program delivery to program growth, each nonprofit discovered that defining and enforcing standards was vital to long-term, sustainable success.

Measuring Performance

In measuring the performance of affiliates, for-profit organizations once again have the benefit of the bottom line, which provides the first signal that performance may be off. Tracking performance is "nothing if not clear," remarked Brue, because "people vote with their feet every day." When the bottom line at a local unit signals a problem, a Bruegger's operator can begin looking for the source of the problem—examining the "people, place, and product" mix set by the national organization—to determine where change is needed. Similarly, MacTemps responded to bottom-line numbers that showed declining sales by introducing new training and quality improvement standards.

In contrast, it is often difficult for nonprofits to develop meaningful performance measures to gauge their progress in dealing with social issues. There is no simple bottom-line, or bottom-line equivalent, for most nonprofits. Moreover, the timing of results is different for nonprofits, where a program's intended effects might not be evident until long after the program is offered. (We don't know, for example, how well a youth program has prepared youth for adulthood until they become adults.)

Compounding these problems is the fact that nonprofit funders, program operators, and clients may all have different views of what constitutes value and, therefore, what to measure. As Stoneman described YouthBuild's stakeholders, she pointed out that the youth may want a program they like, the nonprofit may want a program it believes improves youths' prospects *and* pleases them, but funders may want data about how the program has *changed* youth, a question that can be answered only with complicated evaluations. In the absence of a bottom line, what is the right thing to measure in this scenario—customer satisfaction, program performance against YouthBuild's own goals, or outcomes, as tracked through longer-term evaluation? Many nonprofits seek performance information on all these questions, but their challenge is greater than that of a for-profit using bottom-line figures.

Supporting and Enforcing Performance

All of the national organizations use a combination of support and enforcement to help affiliates meet performance standards. Summerbridge dropped two program operators who were unable or unwilling to deliver the program as specified, and Bruegger's can revoke a franchise for the same reasons. YouthBuild dropped one of the early sites whose director showed divisive tendencies that undermined the network's values. On the other hand, the national organizations provide guidance, such as MacTemp's new quality approaches, to improve performance so it meets specified standards.

TENSIONS IN THE CENTRAL-LOCAL RELATIONSHIP

At the heart of the relationship between local operators and a central organization is a paradox: To get good results in the field, the central entities need entrepreneurial, committed, creative leaders who, almost by definition, will resist direction and control from the central unit.

Managing this tension between field and central operators is a major challenge for any organization growing across multiple sites. How can quality control and "brand protection" be achieved when affiliates, especially the most talented and passionate, are inclined to set their own agendas? The balance revolves around trust and value. Affiliates trust the central entity, and understand the value it provides by insisting on, and supporting, quality performance.

> *To get good results in the field, the central entities need entrepreneurial, committed, creative leaders who, almost by definition, will resist direction and control from the central unit.*

Looking at the central-field tension from a foodservice point of view, Brue describes the central entity's job as one of rejecting innovation from the field, most of the time. Deciding when to adopt something new is risky. On the one hand, "All of the innovation comes up from the bottom, from operators who are closer to the customer, and know what customers want." On the other hand, there would be no end to the number of new ideas generated by a large field of highly motivated operators. The central entity must say no to all ideas until the best ones bounce back enough to signal that it is time to change.

MacTemps describes the tension between the field and central entities as one of trust on the one hand and control on the other. The trust is generated not only from their early policy of expanding through friends, but from a commitment to consistency in *what* the central office gets involved with and *how* it gets involved. Local operators are not subject to unexpected interventions into their operations. Central control is limited to the essentials of supporting profitable performance. MacTemps only has 10 people in its central office, serving 70 retail operations. Synn captures the balance of power between the central office and the field offices by summarizing company policy about adding headcount at headquarters: "It's evil."

YouthBuild USA also engenders trust because it reflects and reinforces the values of its members. One of the fundamental principles of YouthBuild USA—staying close to the grassroots of communities and representing their interests—has fostered an organization that "doesn't act like a national organization." While YouthBuild has kept considerable power centralized in the founder/president, it has gone to great lengths to establish democratic processes to give voice not only to all the programs, but to key constituent groups within the organization, including the youth. Ultimately, Youth-Build USA has no claim on the local operator; its only authorization comes from the associates, who don't *need* the national organization, but continue to *value* it.

CONCLUSION

From loose associations of operators to company-owned stores, and from highly structured to informal management styles, the organizations profiled in this chapter are fundamentally different in a number of ways. Yet all of them discovered the essential character and role of the expansion agent: not only to put new local sites on the map but, more importantly, to sustain a growing number of operators over time. To deliver on that commitment, each developed a set of capacities that would help local operators improve their performance. The national organizations become, in effect, resources for adaptive capacity—the kind that organizations use to learn, innovate, assess and improve quality, and motivate people. While not one reported that developing those capacities was easy, all agreed that the way to expand a program or service was to expand the capacity for local performance.

ORGANIZATION PROFILES

Bruegger's Bagels

P.O. Box 374, Burlington, VT 05402-0374; www.brueggers.com

Founded: 1983

Core business: Franchise bagel shops

Scope: 364 locations in 24 states; 6 commissaries; $210 million sales (1997)

Keys to supporting local performance:

- Beginning with a "franchising mindset"
- Extensive testing to find a winning formula

- Balancing people, product, and place
- Identifying critical success factors
- Focusing the central office on learning, quality improvement, and product development.

"It's important to have someone with a real stake out in the field."

Summerbridge National

1902 Van Ness Avenue, 2nd Floor, San Francisco, CA 94109

Founded: 1978

Core business: Summer study, tutorials, and mentoring for academically talented, underserved middle school students

Scope: 38 programs; $1 million operating budget; 13 employees (1997)

Keys to supporting local performance:

- Taking advantage of the early years to refine and develop ideas
- Insisting on agreement on both broad goals and principles and nonnegotiable details
- Requiring collaboration among the local programs
- Focusing on a signal core objective

"After the long demonstration period, Summerbridge was 'funder ready.' "

MacTemps, Inc.

711 Boylston Street, Boston, MA 02116-2616; www.mactemps.com

Founded: Incorporated in 1986

Core business: Temporary staffing

Scope: 28 U.S. cities, 9 elsewhere; 70 offices; $107 million sales (1997)

Keys to supporting local performance:

- Looking for a "scaleable" concept right from the start
- Creating a strong company culture of trust and cohesion
- A robust testing and training program
- Supporting affiliates through learning, quality assurance, and training

"People still come before systems."

YouthBuild USA

P.O. Box 40322, Somerville, MA 02144; www.youthbuild.org

Founded: 1978, in New York City as Youth Action; YouthBuild USA created in 1988

Core business: Nonprofit support center and intermediary for the YouthBuild movement

Scope: 108 sites in 91 cities across 34 states; 4,600 youth served; $5.5 million operating budget for national intermediary; $5.5 million pass-through via national intermediary; $40 million in direct Housing and Urban Development funds for local operators; additional funds raised by locals and provided by Corporation for National Service (1998)

Keys to supporting local performance:

- Protecting the integrity of the "brand"
- Accepting the tradeoff between discipline and widespread dissemination
- Providing benchmarks for local operators

"A network gives you a sense of greater power, efficacy, and the ability to have an impact."

ADDITIONAL READING

Oster, Sharon M. "Nonprofit Organizations as Franchise Operations," *Nonprofit Management and Leadership*, Vol. 2, No. 3, Spring 1992, pp. 223–238.

Hangstefer, James B. *Creating and Sustaining Company Growth: An Entrepreneurial Perspective for Established Companies*. Waltham, MA: Burton-Merrill, 1997.

ENDNOTES

[1]Carrie Shook, "Frugal Mogul," *Forbes*, July 28, 1997, p. 72

[2]Roland Hodson, "Small, Medium or Large: The Rocky Road to NGO Growth" in Michael Edwards and David Huline, eds., *Making a Difference: NGOS and Development in a Changing World* (London: Earthscan Publications, Ltd., 1992) p. 133.

CHAPTER NINE

Virtuous Capital: Investing in Performance

FRAMING QUESTIONS

▶ How does the foundation funding system influence the structure and priorities of the nonprofit sector and nonprofit organizations?

▶ Why does the venture capital model succeed in getting so many business startups "to scale?"

▶ Could foundations adapt aspects of the venture capital model in the absence of a profit motive?

Although government funders and individual donors provide more funds to nonprofits, foundations often have more influence on nonprofit programs and management. They trade not just in money, with grants totaling $11.8 billion in 1996,[1] but also in ideas. Their support for research, evaluation, and the study of best practices often influences nonprofit practice, particularly when foundations promote the findings through publications and conferences. More often than the nonprofits they support, large foundations have the time and money to develop big-picture strategies. Unfortunately, the big picture at foundations rarely includes concerns about organizational capacity and performance. Even worse, *the day-to-day grantmaking practices of many foundations actually undermine the ability of nonprofits to develop the capacity for sustained high performance.*

The comparison of venture capital and foundation grantmaking that emerged from our inquiry underscores the depth and implications of this problem. More important, it provides a framework for rethinking how grantmaking could support organizational capacity and performance. According to Edward Skloot, executive director of the Surdna Foundation, using venture capital as a metaphor or reference point could inspire foundations "to make a new set of rules to play by."

THE FOUNDATION FUNDING FOCUS: PROGRAM DEVELOPMENT

Although their practices and styles vary, most foundations would probably concur with former Ford Foundation president Franklin Thomas's description of philanthropy as the "research and development arm of society." Especially in the 1960s, there was a tacit if not explicit division of labor among foundations and the public sector. Foundations focused on research and development (R&D). If new ideas proved successful, the federal government would embrace them and assume responsibility for their widespread implementation through government agencies. Many of the signature programs of Lyndon Johnson's Great Society agenda, for example, were developed and tested in demonstrations funded by the Ford Foundation.

Some observers believe that political pressures later drove foundations toward increasingly narrow proposal funding. Peter Frumkin argues that this focus stems from the congressional backlash against foundations, which culminated in a 1969 set of tax reforms that sought to make foundations more accountable. Subsequently, many foundations have focused more sharply on projects and highly specific grant proposals as the basis for funding decisions, rather than organizational or personal reputations.[2]

To carry out this preferred R&D role, foundations organized around program development. Many foundations are known for their key program interests in health, human services, or the environment, for instance, and have actively developed and promoted pace-setting models and initiatives. Grants are given primarily to develop and test new ideas. Few aim to invest in the broader capacities organizations need to sustain and improve the delivery of effective programs.

In the traditional program-centered grantmaking model, the grantor-grantee relationship is shaped by the quest for program innovation. The bulk of a foundation's work comes *before* a grant is made, when the focus is on identifying new program ideas. After the grant is made, the funder usually stays at arm's length, close enough to observe how the program demonstration is proceeding and to ensure that funds are not misappropriated, but often too far away to help in the work of growing a startup.

Some philanthropists and foundations have begun to reexamine this program-centered approach. They are supporting promising entrepreneurs instead of promising programs. But they tend not to distinguish between the skills that an entrepreneur needs to excel at program innovation and the skills needed for management of a growing organization. In the end, they may create more entrepreneurs and more program innovation and still not address the organizational aspects of growth needed for sustainability. Hence the dilemma for the nonprofit sector: It's no one's job to invest in the organizational capacity of nonprofit organizations themselves. Federal funding is shrinking, and with it the possibility of federal scale-up of social ideas. Foundations, meanwhile, continue to operate on a program innovation model.

> *It's no one's job to invest in the organizational capacity of nonprofit organizations themselves.*

THE VENTURE CAPITAL FOCUS: ORGANIZATION BUILDING

Venture capital builds an investment model to serve exactly what the nonprofit sector seeks: innovative ideas and high-performing organizations to get them to market.

171

Unlike most foundations, many early-stage venture capitalists are *not* investing in an untested product or concept. William Bygrave, venture capital researcher and former practitioner, explained that venture capitalists are looking for startups with "evidence of a product." Usually, the product development has already been funded by "the Four F's—founders, families, friends, and the foolhardy." Only then does the venture capitalist enter to help bring an idea with strong sales potential to market.

"We're actually building companies," emphasized Walter Channing, managing partner of CW Group, a leading health-care technology venture firm. He reduced the company-building strategy to a "Four M's formula: management, management, management, and market." Ample management capacity is essential for the early-stage company to respond to the volatile, high-pressure environment of growth. Bob Higgins, managing partner of Highland Capital, explained that with so much change anticipated in the growth environment, it is the management team's ability to respond—not a fixed business plan or strategy—that is decisive. Highland's companies "almost never succeed on their original strategy."

The first step in building a company, venture capitalists agree, is to find the right management talent. Venture capitalists never assume that an entrepreneur will have the right blend of creative genius and management ability needed both to create a product *and* build a company. Most venture capitalists begin by playing an active role in recruiting a CEO. In fact, venture capital deals are often structured so that the growth of a company is not entrusted to the product innovator but instead to a management executive recruited by the venture capitalist. Nor does the venture capitalist's role in building the management team end with recruiting. According to Bygrave's research, upwards of 60 percent of CEOs are replaced over the course of the venture capital investment.

Even at the outset, the company-building process is actually a part of the venture capitalist's exit strategy. The ultimate objective is to sell the startup, either to another company or to investors through an initial public offering (IPO) of stock. In either case, the venture capitalist needs these "take-out" investors to realize a profit. But in order to attract investors, the venture capitalist must first invest in growing the company. The take-out investors are looking for a strong-performing company with good prospects for continued growth and sustainability. There is no exit until the company looks viable.

To enhance the prospects for growth and sustainability, the venture capitalist offers (or imposes) a range of noncash, value-added assistance. This assistance helps the startup reach a series of milestones on the company-building road. At each milestone, the company is visibly stronger, and more attractive to the expanding circle of investors needed to capitalize the next round of growth. It is the venture capitalist's job to help the company find the resources—financial, strategic, and managerial—to define and reach the next milestone. The whole process, which culminates with the IPO, takes an average of five to seven years.

As practiced as a venture capital firm might become at building companies, it always faces high risk. According to Bygrave's rule of thumb for a portfolio of ten investments, two of the deals will be "moon rockets" that produce a big payoff with a successful IPO, and two will end in total failure, with bankruptcy. The rest will be either "walking wounded," which are too weak to get to an IPO but might succeed if the venture capitalist pours more money into them, or "walking dead," which are never strong enough for an IPO yet not so weak they collapse entirely.

As these odds suggest, company-building through venture capital is assumed to be difficult and risky, which explains in part why venture capital represents less than 1 percent of the capital used for startups. The leverage the venture capital deal provides to companies, however, is powerful, with about 30 percent of all companies that succeed and reach the IPO stage backed by venture capital.[3]

COMPARING THE FUNDING MODELS

Six key practices emerge from a comparison of the foundation and venture-capital funding models. (See Exhibit 9-1.) In each case, the venture capital approach stresses building a company to make a product succeed, while the foundation approach stresses narrow investment in a program.

1. *Performance indicators help define success and motivate stakeholders.*

Feature	Venture Capital	Foundation
Performance Indicators How do stakeholders measure success? Who bears the risk of failure? What are the consequences of failure?	Clearly defined goals (building a profitable company), rewards (profit), and risks (financial loss, career setback) for all stakeholders.	Goals hard to define clearly; process measures often substitute for outcomes. Nonprofit's interests (program success, organizational sustainability) different from foundation's (primarily program success). Nonprofits bear more risk.
Exit Strategy When and how does the investor withdraw? Who replaces the initial investor?	From day one, single-minded focus on exit, which is feasible only when prospective buyers judge the company's chances for growth and success to be strong.	Exit not strategic, comes after the program has demonstrated its value; or when funding guidelines impose cut-off. Nonprofit must then solicit other foundations, donors, or rely on fees for service.
Degree of Funding How much of the organization's budget does the investor cover?	Usually a large share, and/or a commitment to help raise additional funds, leaving executives free to manage.	Usually a small share, forcing executives to spend time fundraising.
Duration How long does the investment run?	On average, 5 to 7 years—time required to build a company that can be sold.	Usually 1, 2, or 3 years (rarely longer)—time preferred by foundations.

Terms of Engagement What is the character of the investor-fundee relationship?	Intensive, hands-on partnership aimed at growing the company; "joined at the hip." Sit on board, give advice, get frequent reports, recruit top managers.	More interaction before grant than after the grant. Arm's-length, hands-off oversight aimed at preventing abuses. Focus on program, not organizational outcomes. Reluctant to intervene.
Pace How quickly can the investor respond to changes in the organization's situation?	Investors work on startup's schedule, responding to changes in their environment.	Program officers must work on foundation board schedule; less flexibility to respond to grantees.
Results	For ten investments: 2 stars, 2 failures; 6 "walking dead" or "walking wounded."	Not quantified.
	Only 1 percent of capital for all startups, but back 30 percent of all startups that reach IPO.	Same potential for leverage?

Exhibit 9-1 Venture capital—foundation investment models.

For the major stakeholders in a venture capital investment, success is clearly defined and consistently rewarded. To the venture capitalist, the take-out investor, and the board and management of the startup—all of whom have ownership interests—success means growth and profit. The more capital the startup attracts, and the more market share it captures, the better the chances of a successful IPO, with profits for everyone. The cost of failure, conversely, is also high. A walking-wounded or walking-dead deal means forgone profits. Outright failure means the loss of the investment itself. Too many such deals will scare off the investors who contribute to venture funds, and possibly end in the failure of the venture capital firm itself. Similarly, an individual venture capital associate will be judged on the success of the companies in her portfolio. The same stakes drive the directors and managers of a startup. Consequently, while the odds in the venture capital industry are tough, the incentives to beat them are powerful and consistent.

For the stakeholders in a foundation grant, success is often poorly defined and not consistently rewarded. Having worked in both philanthropy and venture capital, Bob Higgins finds "foundation work ten times more complex than venture capital." The complexity often starts with the problem of defining success. Everyone might agree that success means social impact, but measuring social impact in education reform, youth development, or job training, for example, is implicitly complicated.

Without the benefit of clear performance indicators, many non-profits and their funders use inputs, process, and outputs as surrogates, simply tracking the amount of service provided on the assumption that it makes a difference.

> *The complexity often starts with the problem of defining success. Everyone might agree that success means social impact, but measuring social impact in education reform, youth development, or job training, for example, is implicitly complicated.*

Regardless of how success and failure are gauged, the monetary stakes are not high either way for most grantmakers. Far from worrying about *losing* money, many foundations fret about *spending* enough to meet the IRS mandate for an annual 5 percent payout of their assets. Violators are subject to steep financial sanctions. Program officers' compensation and career prospects, moreover, are not typically tied to the performance of their grantees, over whom they have limited influence.

And unlike a venture capital firm, a foundation can prosper, and even bask in the glow of good works, with little risk of being tarnished by the weak performance of grantees. Annual reports concentrate on grants made, less often on results achieved. So while the odds for success in the nonprofit sector are tough, the risk of failure is not a heavy burden for any single foundation or its staff. "We're not so worried about what our real rate of return is on a particular investment," explained one foundation officer. "We're looking for cumulative returns." This arrangement reduces the pressure to learn and apply lessons quickly to improve performance on the "next round" of grants.

2. *With an exit strategy, a funder withdraws, but leaves behind a stronger organization.*

Paradoxically, the venture capitalist's single-minded focus on exit does not result in a short-term view that inhibits organizational capacity. To the contrary, the capital markets are organized so that the venture capitalist cannot profit until the take-out investors judge the startup's chances for sustained success to be strong. With this sequencing, investment in the company is not terminated when the venture capitalist exits; it is merely transferred through the well-structured mechanism of the IPO to a larger pool of investors.

Frequently, foundations challenge nonprofit organizations to present plans showing how they will sustain their operations after a grant terminates. But without the capital markets of the business world, they can hardly expect a compelling answer. "We have no take-out strategies whatsoever," one grantmaker conceded. "We have high levels of worry and low levels of attention" to this dilemma. Many foundations are able to structure a series of milestones to govern the release of installments over the life of a large grant. Usually, the nonprofit will have to demonstrate a new level of capacity or performance—operating in x number of sites, serving x people, or earning a good evaluation. But there is often no logical point or process for foundations to hand off their investment to others. When a large foundation grant runs out, nonprofit organizations are left to mount a time-consuming search for funds to cover ongoing operation and expansion of programs, from local community foundations, corporate philanthropy, fees for service, and individual donors.

> *Few national foundations want to be take-outs for their peers; because of their devotion to innovation, most want to be in on the ground floor.*

3. *Funding most of an organization's needs enables managers to focus on managing, not raising funds.*

A venture capital firm usually funds a large share of a startup's costs, an arrangement that leaves the CEO free to concentrate on managing the growth of the company. It is the fund originator who has to recruit other investors and then does most of the work managing the investment, drawing on the expertise of other investors as necessary.

A foundation grant, in contrast, tends to cover only a fraction of a nonprofit's costs. Even when a number of grants are combined, most nonprofit organizations are starved for general operating support. "We undercapitalize virtually everything we do," said one foundation officer. As a result, nonprofit executives are forced to spend a large part of their time, sometimes more than half of it, raising money year after year. Compared to a nonprofit executive, a CEO in business has an enormous time advantage, making it possible to focus on managing the organization.

Although the nonprofit sector demands this huge investment in fundraising it simultaneously disinvests in it. Nonprofit managers repeatedly seek technical assistance for fundraising, yet time and resources committed to raising money are generally considered diversions from the delivery of the nonprofit's services.

4. *Building strong organizations takes time.*

On average, it takes venture capital backers of startups five to seven years to move from the initial investment to the sale of the new company. Many deals take longer. Venture capitalists know from collective experience in judging the product, the market, and the penetration necessary to achieve the expected financial results that their efforts will not be short-term.

Nonprofit grantmaking time horizons are dramatically shorter, and are a matter of internal foundation policy more than of practices linked to results. Of the more than 35,000 grants made in 1995 in the five states with the most foundations, only 5.2 percent were for more than one year. On average, the multiyear grants were only 2.5 years in length.[4] Many foundations simply state that they will not fund any program longer than two to three years. Most reason that they do not want to create dependence, or that an idea or organization should prove itself within that time frame.

Many of those nonprofits that do get continuing support in the form of program grants get the grants in one-year installments, with little support for longer-term strategy and a good deal of uncertainty about even their near-term funding prospects. The short grant periods also leave little time for adaptation for the development of programs, processes, or marketing needed to exploit a product or idea. These are the very activities that are essential to the venture capital startup's success. As venture-capitalists say, "It takes five to seven years to raise a plum; two to three to raise a lemon."

5. *Combining money and value-added helps to ensure success.*

Venture capitalists help create success by engaging in the company's work. Investors will often take one or more seats on the company's board to help shape strategy and support a CEO dealing with complicated challenges. "We want the CEO to be able to come in and say, 'Let me tell you how I screwed up this month,'" says Higgins. To supplement formal governance, the venture firm's own "salty entrepreneurs" engage in extensive coaching and mentoring, with "lots of breakfasts and contact outside the board." Bygrave's research shows that the more successful the startup, the more likely it was to have had a board controlled by the venture capital investors.

How valuable is this value-added? In Bygrave's research on 120 entrepreneurs and their venture capital backers, the entrepreneurs gave higher marks for these "soft," value-added services than did the venture capitalists themselves.[5] In the words of one venture-funded executive, "It is far more important *whose* money you get than how much you get or how much you pay for it."[6]

Foundations do see risk in the organization, but respond by assuming an arm's-length *oversight* role that will uncover poor management rather than a *partnering* role that will actively develop capable management. The foundation-grantee relationship is like one of banker and borrower. It hardly encourages startup managers to "come in and tell us how they screwed up." For example, most never take a seat on a nonprofit board. Few become mentors, coaches, or partners. Most program officers, according to one of our foundation executives, are reluctant to get involved with their grantees' organizational problems. They feel it would be a "violation of the trust of the entrepreneur." So while a venture capitalist feels comfortable with the premise that you "won't succeed on your original strategy," foundation staff, as one explained, "feel very uncomfortable" that the value-added grantmaking "might somehow drive someone to do something different from what they originally intended."

Even foundations that do commit to the capacity-building of nonprofit organizations often do so at arm's length. They fund third-party consultants who report only to the nonprofit, not the funder. This arrangement reflects not only the foundation's sensitivity about interference, but also nonprofit managers' fears about exposing organizational weaknesses. For example, Management Consulting Services, a management assistance enterprise funded by several Boston foundations and the United Way of Massachusetts Bay, establishes confidentiality as the first of its operating principles in its work with nonprofits. Similarly, as one nonprofit manager told the Robin Hood Foundation of New York, which has developed a major management assistance initiative as part of its grantmaking, "I'm conscious of a risk just talking to you right now about my management issues."

Finally, the different approaches to engagement are reflected in the workloads carried by the professionals. The typical portfolio for a venture capitalist is five or six companies. The typical foundation officer handles hundreds of grant requests and scores of actual grants each year. Significant structural changes would have to be made for foundations to alter the terms of engagement on a large scale.

> *The typical portfolio for a venture capitalist is five or six companies. The typical foundation officer handles hundreds of grant requests and scores of actual grants each year.*

6. *To be responsive, funders need to work on their investees' timelines.*

In venture capital firms, the principals are also the workers, so decision making keeps pace with events. As conditions change, the company may revise decisions about product choice and volume, physical plant requirements, marketing strategy, size and type of workforce, and of course, management. As anyone who has applied for grants from foundations can attest, deadlines are usually coordinated with the board meetings, because in many foundations the board is the only body with authority to approve grants. (In larger foundations, the executive staff often have a small discretionary fund to make grants.) All foundation activity is paced by the preparation of the "board book." This system is a logical response to the volume of grant requests and the accountability system of board only grants approval. The pace and timing of decision making are established for internal organizational purposes and respond neither to the imperatives of nonprofit organizational issues nor the urgency of public problems.

STRATEGIES FOR CHANGING FOUNDATION PRACTICE

Foundations can use the venture capital approach as a model to develop specific grantmaking strategies or as a framework for rethinking whether and how they can improve the organizational performance of grantees. Literally adopting the model for all grants, however, would surely be inappropriate, and nonprofits would be right to protest if all funders suddenly shifted to an intensive, hands-on grantmaking style for every grant. Particularly with smaller grants (either for the foundation or the nonprofit) and shorter ones (e.g., two years or less), more engaged grantmaking would not seem worth the effort. But a venture approach might be appropriate in cases where the stakes justify special foundation effort—for example, to launch a promising startup, to ramp-up a proven young nonprofit, or to bring depth to a shallow organization with effective programs and potential.

Foundation leaders should take into account some of the benefits that more engaged grantmaking can deliver for the foundation itself. In addition to building the grantee's organizational capacity, such an approach also builds knowledge at the foundation. Greater involvement helps foundations gain a better understanding of front-line conditions, of the real limits and opportunities of the programs they are funding, and of the nature of the public issues the foundation is addressing. Foundations can apply the knowledge and lessons they learn, along with their money, to help grantees on future rounds of funding.

Foundation executives and trustees might ask themselves a few key questions to begin rethinking their approaches.

1. *Is our grant strategy appropriate for the results we're hoping to achieve?*

The best way to determine which investment approach to use is to start with the results the foundation wants. The more specifically the desired result can be formulated, the easier it will to be support the grantee with an appropriate style of grantmaking. Sweeping social-change goals will need to be converted into a series of clear, interim results that the grantee and funder can work toward together.

The GE Fund's College Bound initiative provides a good example of setting clear goals and choosing grantmaking strategies to support them. The Fund's goal for an education improvement program is to increase the number of college-bound students in the public school systems in towns with GE facilities. That goal led the

Fund logically into new relationships with its grantees. Most strikingly, the Fund is committed for the long haul. As long as the principal is leading the school in new efforts and there are signs of improvement, the Fund will stay with the school (up to seven years and counting in one case). GE employees are closely involved in student mentoring, adding additional value to the grant. Although the work takes longer and involves more foundation effort, the results have been gratifying, with one school boosting the percentage of college-bound students from 25 to 75 percent.

As a recently issued report of the National Committee for Responsive Philanthropy details, a number of leading conservative foundations have developed remarkably coherent and effective grantmaking strategies to effect a major change in public policy.[7] The major features of their grantmaking practices are:

- Focus on building institutions—with 36 percent of total grants going to unrestricted general operating support
- Concentration in relatively few institutions, each of which received significant support
- Very clearly articulated objectives for their public policy grantmaking
- Focus on networks of institutions that can affect change comprehensively
- Long-term commitments to the objectives and institutions

With a long-term but clearly articulated goal of changing public policy, the funders chose strategies that departed from conventional grantmaking but are credited with high impact.

2. *Are we close enough to grantees to become partners in problem-solving?*

Just as program officers are beginning to work more closely with nonprofits and communities to design more relevant social programs, so they should be getting closer on organizational issues. To get new results they will have to overcome the traditional arm's-length response to organizational challenges. Typically, a foundation funds a third-party consultant to help the nonprofit, while program officers remain largely uninvolved and interested mostly in short-term program outcomes. Handing the work off to a third-party consultant limits the chances for funders and grantees to discover how organizational capacity can drive program impact. The more funders understand the complexity and challenges of organizational work, and shoulder some of the burden and risk, the better they will be able to support effective organization-building strategies that improve programs.

New American Schools (NAS), funded with grants from corporations, foundations, and philanthropists, is essentially a venture capital vehicle established to give young school-reform programs what most foundations cannot: large grants over a long period of time in conjunction with formal and informal assistance to grow and expand the programs. Led by John Anderson (a former IBM executive) and a board of corporate CEOs and leading educators, NAS staff are close enough to their grantees to make judgments in consultation with them about what kind of help to offer—coaching or consulting assistance, for example—and exactly what results the grantees should be held accountable for. The capacity-building is explicitly understood as a means of delivering and growing programs with real impact, and is not a marginal enterprise. The depth of the relationship (NAS works with only seven programs) enables NAS to act more like a venture capitalist than a foundation.

As a next step in integrating grantmaking and organization-building, foundations might consider establishing operations like NAS's, but *within* their own organizations. The proximity of such an effort to the foundation's program officers and trustees would help overcome the fragmented learning that takes place when organization-building is decoupled from grantmaking. Even if program officers are not going to match the depth of such an operation's involvement, they stand to learn a great deal, which can help them add more value to their grantees's work.

Unfortunately, current tax policy may discourage foundations from integrating an expensive resource like this within their organizations. By setting up a new entity, foundations can fund it through grants, which can be counted toward the IRS-mandated annual payout of 5 percent of their assets. To establish it internally, for all the value it creates, will simply make the foundation's operating overhead appear larger.

Some corporate foundations may have an advantage in integrating organizational and program goals. Venture capital firms and management consulting companies, for example, are experienced in building strong organizations. Participants in our roundtable discussion suggested setting up a philanthropic venture fund within a venture capital firm and assigning venture capitalists to work pro bono with nonprofits in leveraging grants through organization building. Management consultancies, many of which already do pro bono work as well as making some grants, could similarly combine the two.

The Community Foundation for Greater New Haven has begun to change its practices to support closer partnerships with grantees receiving especially large grants. The Foundation is developing and testing policy guidelines that permit the staff to take seats on the boards of grantee organizations. (Considerations include the size of their investment relative to the total budget, the nature of the grant, the overall condition of the organization, and the role or purpose of membership itself.)

In 1990, The Roberts Foundation established the Homeless Economic Development Fund to provide support to nonprofit organizations that establish businesses employing homeless people. The strategy was to invest large sums in a relatively small number of enterprises, giving the foundation enough leverage and the organizations enough capital to improve the chances for success. Jed Emerson, the fund's director, became closely involved in all of the enterprises, learning and coaching as the enterprises grew.

3. *Is our grantmaking portfolio appropriately balanced between grants for program innovation and organization building?*

Foundations are making mostly targeted grants that support specific programs. According to *Foundation Giving*, general support grants (which are not restricted to the operation of a specific program) represented only about 15 percent of total grants in 1993, down from 25 percent in 1980. Program grants, meanwhile, have grown from just over 30 percent of all grants made in 1980 to 45 percent in 1993. Foundations need to determine whether they are too invested in program support to support organizational capacity.

As a recent Conservation Company report to the New York Community Trust[8] recommended, funders interested in organizational capacity might define new categories of grant—something between totally unrestricted general support and highly targeted program grants. These "organization grants" could specify outcomes for capacity building and invest appropriately. They would create the discipline and outcomes for capacity-building that grants now often demand for programs.

In Boston, for example, several foundations have joined with the local United Way and the state Department of Public Health to try a new approach to organization-building. They have funded the Common Ground project, an intensive, three-year program for 17 multiservice, community-based organizations. The funders consider these organizations essential to improving the prospects of several distressed neighborhoods, and have therefore committed to investments that will take organization-strengthening beyond the traditional quick-fix of an organizational assessment followed by a short consultation. Instead, Common Ground will offer these organizations ongoing training and professional development, backed up by longer-term consulting resources to help them implement new approaches. The funders recognize that stronger organizations will ultimately determine how successful the programs are.

On a related question of portfolio balance, foundations might consider whether they are too wedded to *early-stage* funding of programs. Many could give support at later stages, when a program or organization is at a critical juncture, but other foundations have already invested and left. Later-stage funding, combined with a focus on organizational capacity, could help nonprofits sharpen their impact.

4. *Do we as a foundation have the capacity to invest differently?*

The idea of a resource-constrained foundation seems like an oxymoron, but program officers at most foundations are already stretched thin just building and managing their existing portfolios responsibly. To pay more than lip service to a new investment approach, foundation management and boards will need to reassess their own capacity for a hands-on, organization-centered approach. They will have to conquer the traditional nonprofit overhead phobia and consider how they might expand their own organizational capacity and/or restructure their grantmaking operations. Larger foundations may find it more difficult than smaller ones to adjust to the higher level of staff or consultant time required of these investments.

Foundations might also consider how to balance the program and policy expertise of their staffs with new organizational skills. Many would need additional staff with more experience in organization-building to ensure that intelligent bets are made, strong strategies are developed, and that the foundation's value-added is in fact helpful. To recruit for this skill-set, foundations would have to buck the trend to "professionalize" the program officer position. People with varied backgrounds, in business, institution-building, and consulting, would add new depth to a new approach.

As a central part of its mission, the Robin Hood Foundation provides management assistance to the organizations it supports, which has led it to include former management consultants on its staff. It provides assistance both from in-house staff as well as paid and pro-bono professionals. They make general operating grants that are renewable year after year without time limit. They have funded up to 50 percent of organization's operating budgets. They have engaged in intensive planning and problem-solving with their grantees. This work has not been without its challenges. Deputy Director Lisa Smith reports, "We are learning that true venture capital practices in the not-for-profit arena are even more resource intensive than we thought." But with the right staff, the chances of succeeding are better.

STRATEGIES FOR CHANGING NONPROFIT PRACTICE

Like the foundations that support them, nonprofit organizations need to reconsider their approach to capacity-building. Many have been conditioned by the existing grant-seeking process to camouflage their organizational expenses and needs, which they cover by charging small amounts of overhead to multiple grants. Nonprofits need to ask, "Assuming foundations *were* more responsive to our organizational needs, what would we propose to do?" Even if foundations are not offering, there is nothing to stop determined nonprofits from articulating a compelling organizational strategy and asking foundations to invest.

1. *Are we defining our organizational needs for funders?* Most nonprofits would put general operating support, or unrestricted grants, at the top of the wish list. But to get more support for organizational needs, nonprofits will have to articulate a clear agenda that outlines a disciplined plan for using the nonprogram money and show how, ultimately, it will enhance program impacts. Instead of worrying about exposing their organizational weaknesses, the nonprofits will have to sell weaknesses by explaining that they know where to strengthen their organizations and can deploy resources efficiently and strategically to get the job done.

    For example, when Family Service America mounted a fundraising campaign to help its 250 member nonprofits adopt new community-centered approaches, it didn't pitch a new model program. Instead, it laid out an analysis of the organizational needs—from training and change management to staff recruiting and benchmarking—and got foundations to invest in these organizational strengthening programs as a way of driving program outcomes.

> *Instead of worrying about exposing their organizational weaknesses, nonprofits will have to* sell *weaknesses by explaining that they know where to strengthen their organizations and can deploy resources efficiently and strategically to get the job done.*

2. *Are we selective about the foundations we want as partners?* While the tendency in fundraising is to go after any relevant grant, getting into an intensive partnership with the wrong venture-

style funder is likely to mean wasted effort and considerable angst. Even cash-starved business startups are often selective about whose venture capital money they seek. They know they will be partners with the investor, interacting frequently to make difficult decisions. Nonprofits looking for value-added funding need to communicate clearly where they are trying to take the organization; establish expectations that the funder will share risk and burdens; and create a plan that demands value-added support from a funder. Beware foundations that have simply repositioned themselves under a venture capital banner but lack the capacity, willingness, and patience to do the gritty work of venture capital. Indeed, the foundations that have begun to develop more engaged grant-making are learning that patience and adaptation are critical.

3. *Are we showing foundations a clear plan that justifies longer-term support?* Nonprofits need to work with foundations to develop an exit strategy that identifies some "take-out" funders. In a sector starved for capital, and with no IPO to produce an infusion of cash, this challenge may be the most difficult aspect of longer-term engagement. But nonprofits need to focus on how they might tap new funding sources, and propose that early funders stay with them until they reach that point.

One organization that used this approach is Cooperative Home Health Care (CHCA), a worker-owned cooperative in the Bronx that provides health care to the elderly in their homes. The cooperative has proved quite successful: it offers home health aides attractive pay, working hours, and benefits, and it offers the community high-quality services. Because of its success, CHCA wanted to expand its operations and launch a training institute to create new cooperatives. When it approached a previous funder, the Charles Stewart Mott Foundation in Flint, Michigan, CHCA presented a long-term plan for building self-sustaining cooperatives. The Mott Foundation subsequently made a series of renewable grants over a seven-year period. Programs such as CHCA's provide a clear incentive for funders to move away from traditional terms of one or two years toward the longer-term grants that can have sustained impact.

CONCLUSION

The venture capital model, after years of practice, competition, and refinement, has emerged as a comprehensive investment strategy. Each venture capital practice complements the others, and all support consistent performance objectives. Foundation grantmaking practices (which determine the size and length of grants and the grantor-grantee relationship) have emerged to support foundations in their R&D role. But do those practices consistently yield the value foundations now seek—sustainable, improved conditions for our society? Unfortunately, there is no data to suggest that this model succeeds in bringing a significant number of social ideas to scale. Venture capital is a tiny percentage of total investment in startups, but provides for a large proportion of those startups that get to scale through IPOs. Could foundations, which likewise are a small proportion of funding for nonprofits, use new investment practices to produce similar results for the nonprofit sector?

ADDITIONAL READING

Bygrave, William D. and Jeffrey A. Timmons. *Venture Capital at the Crossroads*. Boston: Harvard Business School Press, 1992.

Emerson, Jed, and Fay Twersky, eds. *New Social Entrepreneurs: The Success, Challenge and Lessons of Nonprofit Enterprise Creation*. San Francisco: Roberts Foundation, 1996.

Frumkin, Peter. "Private Foundations as Public Institutions," in *Studying Philanthropic Foundations: New Scholarship, New Possibilities* by Ellen Condliffe Lagemann, ed. Bloomington: Indiana University Press, 1988.

Lerner, Josh. "A Note on the Venture Capital Industry." Harvard Business School Publishing, 1994.

Sahlman, William Andrew. *Insights from Venture Capital Organizations*. Boston: Division of Research, Harvard Business School, 1991.

ENDNOTES

[1] American Association of Fund-Raising Counsel Trust for Philanthropy, *Giving USA* (Norwalk, CT: 1997).

[2] Peter Frumkin, "Private Foundations as Public Institutions" in *Studying Philanthropic Foundations: New Scholarship, New Possibilities*, Ellen Condliffe Lagemann, ed. (Indiana University Press: 1988).

[3] Josh Lerner, "A Note on the Venture Capital Industry" (Boston: Harvard Business School Publishing, 1994.)

[4] *Foundation Grants Index 1996* (New York: Foundation Center, 1997)

[5] William D. Bygrave and Jeffrey A. Timmons, *Venture Capital at the Crossroads* (Boston: Harvard Business School Press, 1992), p. 217.

[6] Bygrave and Timmons, p. 208.

[7] Sally Covington, *Moving a Public Policy Agenda: The Strategic Philanthropy of Conservative Foundations*. (Washington, DC: National Committee for Responsive Philanthropy, 1997).

[8] Michael Seltzer and Joseph Stillman, *Strengthening New York City Nonprofit Organizations: A Blueprint for Action* (New York: The Conservation Company, 1994).

CHAPTER TEN

Building a Nonprofit Agenda for Performance

What would it take to turn the tide in the nonprofit sector, so that nonprofit leaders are not forced to manage upstream? So that funding, policy, board priorities, and organizational cultures supported, rather than thwarted, the efforts of managers to create high performing organizations? To achieve that, the nonprofit sector will need to mobilize behind an agenda that promotes organizational performance as a critical resource for creating large-scale social impact. To develop that resource, in turn, will involve more education, research, and investment in and about the organizational capacity needed for high performance. The agenda will need to appeal to a broad constituency—managers, boards, funders, academics, policy makers—but the work will have to begin with nonprofit managers and boards who are willing to learn and proclaim what it really takes for a nonprofit organization to be effective.

WHY AN ORGANIZATIONAL PERFORMANCE AGENDA?

Before they create and advance a performance agenda, nonprofit stakeholders will need to address the question of why we need such an agenda in the first place. They will need to make performance more compelling by linking it to the missions and values that non-profits do honor. Performance may look like a marginal issue, for example, to those who see the nonprofit sector primarily as a venue for expressing commitment to a social cause. Performance may also look marginal to those who see the nonprofit sector as a venue where citizens work collectively, creating the civic and democratic bonds that hold society together. For people who value the nonprofit sector for these ends, organizational capacity and performance may seem more relevant for others—management enthusiasts or bureaucrats.

In reality, however, performance is all about translating caring, believing, and compassion into results. And most nonprofits will find that they pay a price, in both mission and values, by neglecting the organizational capacity needed to get those results. Ultimately, nonprofits make commitments to advance a cause *on society's behalf, with society's money* (in the form of charity, government grants, contracts, and tax subsidies to philanthropy). Far from threatening these goals, organizational capacity—including the management processes discussed in this book—enables nonprofits to live up to these commitments. Specifically, it helps nonprofits hold themselves accountable to their clients, their employees, and their funders.

Accountability to Clients and Communities

If a nonprofit assumes responsibility for service to others in the community, but has no methods for assessing the quality of that service, can it really be accountable to its constituents? Several of the processes we have explored—for example, benchmarking, quality systems, and program development—are all aimed at identifying opportunities to improve services or create new programs that better serve the nonprofit's constituents. These three processes illustrate how organizational capacity can actually help a nonprofit honor its values and deliver on its mission. They highlight where and how people and communities can be better served. A nonprofit that obligates itself to higher standards as part of its mission will go to the trouble of using such approaches. A nonprofit that goes to that trouble can be considered truly accountable to its clients and community.

Accountability to Employees and Volunteers

What does a nonprofit owe its employees and volunteers? There are several benefits if we consider the deal that nonprofits and their employees often make implicitly. The nonprofit is giving its employees the opportunity to work on issues that they find socially important and personally appealing. In many places, the nonprofit is also granting them an opportunity to work in an organization free of what many at least imagine to be the more stifling aspects of corporate culture. Many employees believe things may be more open, less cut-throat, perhaps more collegial and trusting in a nonprofit. But weighed against what many nonprofit workers give up in return, these benefits begin to pale. Many work long hours for low salaries, try to develop their careers in organizations that do not offer many opportunities for advancement, and deal with nearly intractable social problems where progress is hard to make and measure. There are good reasons why nonprofits have so many burnout casualties.

Nonprofit organizations cannot change all of these conditions, but they can change some of them. The human resources strategies and program development strategies that we discussed are two approaches for making fundamental changes. Effective human resources strategies are not concerned primarily with money, but with designing jobs so that employees can produce results and see those results. By improving job satisfaction and developing employees, these strategies can help an organization make a better deal with its employees. Similarly, the best program development strategies are aimed at supporting the ability of employees to be creative, to get good ideas from constituents, and to work together to generate effective service or product ideas. They help employees do better work, and feel better about work.

Accountability to Funders

We have focused elsewhere on the burdens and obstacles that funders often impose on nonprofits, making it difficult for nonprofits to build effective organizations. These funder-created problems notwithstanding, nonprofits still have a deep obligation to be accountable to funders. While grant awards and funding contracts often stipulate specific points on which the nonprofit will be held accountable, there is a larger dimension to funder accountability. Put simply, Is the money well spent? Is the nonprofit efficient? Are its programs effective? Are programs improved and replaced as the organization learns more from the research literature, from constituents, and from its own experience? Is the organization harnessing employees' talents by challenging and supporting them? It is possible to meet the letter of a grant-award or contract and miss the spirit of these larger questions. But nonprofits can, and some do, use organizational processes that ensure that funds are well spent.

Organizational capacity, then, can be a powerful resource that enables a nonprofit organization to honor its mission and values by obligating itself to perform better for its constituents, its staff, and its funders. The capacity building processes refined by the organizations profiled in this book—nonprofit and for-profit alike—are not only compatible with nonprofits' operational needs, but also with their social missions. When these processes are used together, they begin to change not only the results but also the culture of the organization. People begin to see how performance and mission go hand-in-hand. They are willing to tackle the challenges of improving performance because it will help them deliver their services with integrity and effectiveness.

If this accountability rationale alone is not compelling, more and more nonprofits may become interested in organizational capacity as a matter of survival. As research by Joseph Galaskiewicz and Wolfgang Bielefeld[1] indicates, nonprofits that develop their management capacity attract more grants, employees, and volunteers. Those that offer services for fees also attract more fees.

> *Some observers of philanthropy have argued that better capacity and performance may make donors more confident and therefore more willing to make more or bigger grants.*

These findings are especially important news for the many non-profits, mostly in social services, that find themselves competing with for-profit companies that have often focused more on building both their capacity and their capital base. In the marketplace for public contracts, government decision makers are increasingly focused on performance and results. While they may appreciate and share the values of service, compassion, and caring that non-profits bring to their work, they are increasingly paying for the outcomes that organizations provide. Developing the capacity for performance may not only be a matter of enhancing accountability, but of surviving.

WHAT IS AN AGENDA FOR ORGANIZATIONAL PERFORMANCE?

An organizational performance agenda would not aim at prescribing new tools and practices for use by nonprofit managers, but at challenging all stakeholders in the sector to think differently about organizational capacity. It would mobilize managers, funders, and researchers to define and test the value of organizational capacity in delivering social results. (This book, in fact, represents one such hypothesis; i.e., that nonprofits can use organizational processes to improve their performance and results.) An organizational performance agenda would, moreover, identify the assets and obstacles that would need to be mobilized or overcome in order to create a sector more conducive to organizational performance.

Can such an agenda be developed in a decentralized, pluralistic environment as broad as the nonprofit sector? Recent experiences in business and government suggest that a multitude of players, by testing and embracing some fundamental ideas, can converge to effect broad-scale change. In business, many corporations have developed and promoted an agenda that supports the creation of "high-performance organizations," where boards, managers, and employees use a range of organizational strategies and practices to improve productivity, competitiveness, and the nature of jobs themselves. Aided by researchers, consultants, and public policy makers, a growing number of businesses have advanced the core idea that organizations can be redesigned to enhance their own prospects for success and, therefore, those of the American economy.[2]

More recently, but just as profoundly, the public sector at all levels has been collectively advancing a "reinventing government" agenda that aims to improve the performance of public agencies—in terms of efficiency, effectiveness, and responsiveness—and, in the process, restore the legitimacy and leadership of government agencies. The agenda, which started with a conviction that new approaches were needed, and then advanced to a series of experiments with new practices, has now been supported by public policy, legislation, regulation, and the development of new management strategies. As a result, government is conducting its business differently.[3] The nonprofit sector is facing its own crisis of legitimacy and effectiveness. It can respond by wrapping itself in the nonprofit flag—preaching the social virtues of volunteers, compassion, and service—or it can begin to search for additional leverage in solving social problems.

Ultimately, it is nonprofit managers and boards who will have to lead the way in setting an agenda and rallying people around it. And as all the cases in our inquiry illustrate, it will be individual leaders who begin advancing that agenda by challenging organizations to develop their organizational capacity. They are the ones who now carry the burden of "managing upstream," trying to build effective organizations in an unsupportive environment. No other stakeholders are therefore as likely to be as motivated as managers and boards in taking this lead. They will need to experiment with new organizational processes that could produce better results, and then assess what type of support is needed to advance their work. With a case that links organizational performance and results, they can then start pressing their case with funders. They need to tell the world what it takes to build and sustain a strong organization.

Funders also belong in the vanguard of promoting new ideas and practices for performance. If funders conclude that organizational capacity is a compelling challenge, they have to begin to integrate it into their programmatic work. All program officers, board members, and staff will need to explore how organizational capacity can deliver results. They need to begin to appreciate what many of the leaders running nonprofits understand: that organizational effectiveness drives program outcomes, and that the two are inextricably linked.

> *The nonprofit sector is facing its own crisis of legitimacy and effectiveness. It can respond by wrapping itself in the nonprofit flag— preaching the social virtues of volunteers, compassion, and service—or it can begin to search for additional leverage in solving social problems.*

How should foundations respond to this knowledge? Ideally, the responses should vary, according to the strengths and capacities of the foundation. The worst outcome would be a stampede to a new conventional wisdom, whereby all foundations begin going through the motions of supporting organizational capacity without first discovering what the issue really means for their grantees and how they can best support it. Instead, foundations should explore how to build on their current interests and practices, so that organizational capacity becomes a resource for advancing their social goals.

As a first step in helping organizations build their capacity for performance, foundations need to focus on their own capacity for performance. They could start by asking themselves what a high-performing foundation might look like. They could then consider how much they invest in their own adaptive capacity—the systems for learning, innovation, quality, and motivation that help an organization perform. Most will probably conclude that they are not expert in the many organizational processes that ensure accountability to clients, staff, and benefactors. This should prompt them to ask of themselves the same questions they ask of grantees—"Are we accountable? Are we getting results?" And they are as likely as nonprofits to worry about expanding staff if it makes "overhead" look big, regardless of the benefits such investments might yield. As they reach out to support grantees, they will have to enlarge their own understanding of and experience with these issues.

THE ROLE OF RESEARCHERS AND EDUCATORS

As the growing number of university degree programs and research centers suggest, nonprofits are attracting more attention from researchers and educators. Some of this growing interest should be focused on the role of organizational capacity and performance. While management courses catering to nonprofit practitioners are becoming plentiful, more fundamental questions about organizational capacity and performance remain neglected. For example, How are organizational performance and social impact related? Can we document the outcomes of management processes? How do business practices need to be adapted in order to be useful to nonprofit organizations? Professional education and development curricula could be expanded to help staff succeed not only in the practice of their own profession or discipline but also in the development of management and organizational processes that support effective programs. As educators, social workers, community developers, and advocates of all sorts focus on this link between performance and mission, continuing education within the sector could become a significant resource for supporting large-scale social impact. Much more could be offered about organizational processes aimed specifically at supporting innovation, motivating employees, measuring and improving performance, and so on.

Working together, nonprofit practitioners and researchers could begin to develop a "theory of practice" that will help nonprofits understand how organizational capacity can support performance. While nonprofits excel at convening and communicating about any number of programmatic and social agendas, they give much less attention to a discussion of their own organizational strategies and needs. And it is nearly impossible to advance the use of better organizational processes when managers and staff do not understand the rationale and potential—the theory—behind them. Nonprofits that explore how specific processes can drive outcomes are likely to pursue them much more aggressively. And as more nonprofits engage each other in discussion and learning about these processes and their fundamental values, they can begin to raise the visibility and support for them.

CONCLUSION

The challenge for nonprofit organizations is to build strong organizations without compromising their commitment to social goals. The key to making organizational capacity a means to social ends is to use management processes that enhance responsiveness to clients and support quality improvements, and not just those that enhance appeal to funders. It is also essential to build on the assets of nonprofit organizations in implementing new organizational processes. Though we have tended to focus on many of the obstacles that nonprofits face in using organizational processes, many have also used the traditional interests and culture of the nonprofit sector to their advantage. Distinctive nonprofit assets—including commitment to service, teamwork, and employee empowerment—can give nonprofits important advantages in building better organizations that produce better outcomes.

For example, most nonprofits have a strong service culture and lack only the tools to measure and improve their services more effectively, so that their performance matches their commitment. Similarly, many nonprofits have a commitment to teamwork and collaboration in the workplace, which many observers deride as indecisiveness and process for its own sake. Yet this commitment to teamwork is central to many of the business approaches that are helping organizations achieve better results. The nonprofits that have learned to channel the commitment to teamwork, linking it to well defined objectives and processes that get the most out of teams, have important assets. Another nonprofit asset is the widespread commitment to employee empowerment—the centerpiece of many human resources, quality improvement, and product development approaches.

> *Distinctive nonprofit assets—including commitment to service, teamwork, and employee empowerment—can give nonprofits important advantages in building better organizations that produce better outcomes.*

What is needed is a commitment to build on these assets, converting them from cultural preferences into organizational processes that create results, and integrating those processes into a culture that values social outcomes and organizational performance. The ability of nonprofit leaders to mobilize society for change is another of these distinctive nonprofit assets. Nonprofit leaders now need to leverage that ability to improve their own prospects. Like many of the challenges nonprofits face, mobilizing the sector behind a high-performance agenda is long-term work. There is no final destination, only a continuum of achievement. It begins with exploring, testing, investing in and expanding the capacity of nonprofit organizations for high performance.

ADDITIONAL READING

Appelbaum, Eileen and Rosemary Batt. *The New American Workplace*. Ithaca, NY: ILR Press, 1994.

Osborne, David and Ted Gaebler, *Reinventing Government: How the Entrepreneurial Spirit is Transforming the Public Sector*. Reading, MA: Addison-Wesley, 1992.

Spears, Larry C., ed. *Reflections on Leadership: How Robert K. Greenleaf's Theory of Servant-leadership Influenced Today's Top Management Thinkers*. New York: John Wiley & Sons, 1995.

ENDNOTES

[1] Joseph Galaskiewicz and Wolfgang Bielefeld, *Nonprofit Organizations in an Age of Uncertainty: A Study of Organizational Change* (Forthcoming, Aldine de Gruyter).

[2] For a good review of the theory, practice, and policy associated with the "high-performance work organization" in the private sector, see Eileen Appelbaum and Rosemary Batt, *The New American Workplace* (Ithaca, NY: ILR Press, 1994).

[3] David Osborne and Ted Gaebler, *Reinventing Government: How the Entrepreneurial Spirit is Transforming the Public Sector* (Reading, MA: Addison-Wesley, 1992).

Index